LINCOLN CHRISTIAN COLLEGE AND SEMINARY

P9-DFI-420

THE SPECTACLE OF WORSHIP IN A WIRED WORLD

THE SPECTACLE OF WORSHIP IN A WIRED WORLD

Electronic Culture
and the
Gathered People of God

Tex Sample

ABINGDON PRESS
Nashville

THE SPECTACLE OF WORSHIP IN A WIRED WORLD
ELECTRONIC CULTURE AND THE GATHERED PEOPLE OF GOD

Copyright © 1998 by Tex Sample

All rights reserved.

No part of this work may be reproduced or transmitted in any form or by any means, electronic or mechanical, including photocopying and record-ing, or by any information storage or retrieval system, except as may be expressly permitted by the 1976 Copyright Act or in writing from the publisher. Requests for permission should be addressed in writing to Abingdon Press, 201 Eighth Avenue South, P. O. Box 801, Nashville, TN 37202, U.S.A.

This book is printed on acid-free, recycled paper.

Library of Congress Cataloging-in-Publication Data
The spectacle of worship in a wired world : electronic culture and the gathered people of God / Tex Sample.
     p. cm.
    Includes index.
    ISBN 0–687–08373–7 (pbk. : alk. paper)
    1. Church work with young adults. 2. Young adults—United States–religious life. 3. Baby boom generation. 4. Generation X. 5. Mass media–Religious aspects–Christianity. 6. Popular culture–Re-ligious aspects–Christianity. 7. Liturgics. I. Title.
BV4446.S25   199 8
261.5'2–dc21
                                   98-34585
                                       CIP

Unless otherwise noted, all scripture quotations are from The New Re-vised Standard Version Bible, copyright © 1989 by the Division of Christian Education of the National Council of the Churches of Christ in the USA. Used by permission.

00 01 02 03 04 05 06 07— 10 9 8 7 6 5 4

MANUFACTURED IN THE UNITED STATES OF AMERICA

15-21

To
Blake Emilio Butler
Hailey Jo Butler
Melissa Nagakura Sample
Jessica Mai Sample

95296

CONTENTS

ACKNOWLEDGMENTS

I am indebted to a host of people, many of whom I cannot name. I met them all across the United States as I have lectured on the topic of this book. So many people taught me as I worked with them in church basements and sanctuaries, hotels, conferences, retreat centers, colleges, and seminaries.

My estimate is that I have lectured on these questions of electronic culture more than two hundred times in the last four years. People teach you a great deal in that much time. I owe them all; I only wish I could be as faithful to their contributions as they were to my learning.

Some deserve special note. Larry Hollon was especially important in reading the manscript as I wrote it. His expertise in filmmaking brought to the work the wisdom of one practiced in the arts that are discussed here. Mollie Smith extended my acquaintance with contemporary Christian music and worship. Brian Q. Newcomb gave needed help on rock music. Emanuel Cleaver III was the resident authority on rap music. Harry Foockle, Yolanda Villa Ward, and Susan Chinnery—my pastors—read and commented on the manuscript. Marsha McFee instructed me about dance. Mary Jane Shewmake, my student assistant, provided help with text, bibliography, endnotes, and index. Margaret Kohl, faculty secretary, gave her fine skills as well as her gracious person. Jonathan Arnpriester, who practices the forms of worship sought here, gave the manuscript an experienced reading. Marsha Morgan, professor of theater at Park College, instructed me and shared her own creative work in drama and worship. Gene and Sarah Lowry provided their ever helpful reading and response to the manuscript. William B. McClain engaged me in a spirited conversation about the manuscript on a very helpful summer evening.

The students at Saint Paul School of Theology are close to my heart and I am enormously indebted to them. They are unfailingly patient when I work on these things in class. Their steady teaching about the various musics at work in the larger society, particularly among the young, is desperately needed by one like me encoded and wired from an earlier time. I am aware of the very different way they "converge" the world, and I envy their "naturalness" with things electronic.

I am indebted to the administration, faculty, and staff of Saint Paul who provide daily stimulation and support for the work I do. It is an extraordinary community in which to work. I cannot imagine a theological school that takes the academy, the church, and the society with more seriousness and devotion. It has been my honor and pleasure to teach there for thirty-one years.

Our grandchildren now grow up in a world very different from the one we knew. We hope desperately that they will find the Christian faith and the church the sources of strength and aspiration they have been in our lives. The greatest reward of a work like this would be if it made a small contribution to the witness of the church to the millions of people born since World War II for whom image, beat, and visualization have shaped their knowing, their feelings, their senses, their very lives. This work is dedicated to our grandchildren in the hope that the church can make the shift to the new world forming before our very eyes, ears, and embodied selves.

Finally I cannot hope to measure the contribution of Peggy Sample. She is the one who keeps up with the various artists and theater presentations in town. She gets the tickets and schedules the opportunities to see Willie Nelson, Tina Turner, the symphony, *La Bohème, Smokey Joe's Cafe, Joseph and the Amazing Technicolor Dreamcoat, Les Misérables, Phantom of the Opera, Godspell, Jesus Christ Superstar,* and "The Judds' Farewell Tour." Peggy is the one who provides a steady flood of wonderful music from a broad range of genres in our home. Because of her we take in performances at the Bolshoi in Moscow, the floor show at the Galata Tower in Istanbul, "The Will Rogers Follies" in New York, and the "Stomp" production in Kansas City. She initiates and sustains our friendships with artists and musicians and keeps us on the road to the museums and art galleries that so enrich our lives. Her informed and broad musical, dramatic, and artistic taste teaches me every day. Sometimes I feel that our very house sings!

CHAPTER ONE

Electronic Culture and the Reconstruction of Our Lives

Larry Hollon is a filmmaker and video producer. He won the Cine Golden Eagle Award, was once nominated for an Emmy, and has been honored otherwise any number of times. So he is good. Several years ago he was invited by a nonprofit organization to do a recruitment video for them. This organization recruits college graduates who agree to work on humane projects in the Third World for subsistence wages.

They said, "Larry, we want you to go to Ghana and videotape our entire effort over there and come home and put it into a five-minute tape."

"Oh, my," responded Larry, "you can't do that. It's too much to get into a five-minute tape."

"Larry, it has to be five minutes. We show these tapes in student centers on college campuses. We can't get a college student to watch a recruitment video for more than five minutes."

After some conversation regarding his skepticism about the length of the tape, Larry finally agreed to give it his best shot. He spent three weeks in Ghana and did thirty hours of taping while there. When he came home, he went to work cutting it down to five minutes. When he had finished the editing, he invited me to view the tape and offer my opinion.

We set a date, and I showed up at the appointed time. Larry took me into his studio, which is a bank of electronic machinery that takes up two sizable walls. I sat down on the couch and waited while he pulled out a videotape and pushed it into a slot in one of the machines.

The tape started. It is difficult to describe it in words. It flashed from one scene to another in rapid fashion. Larry, of course, has these very tasteful techniques in which one scene dissolves in particles on the screen only to have another form out of that debris. Then the camera moved to a focus point on the screen only to expand into yet another scene. These and other approaches struck me unexpectedly and moved me quickly through the video. Sometimes one person talked and then another person took up the narrative and continued it.

But all this is taking place with vigorous rapidity. I become aware that I am actually breathing hard. I'm an old baseball pitcher, never a very good one, but I feel as if I have been running wind sprints. As I watch Larry's tape I am breathing hard and my heart is pumping!

The tape ends in what seems like a minute.

"Gadzooks, Larry, that thing is quick. I'm actually breathing hard just from watching it! I feel as if I've been running."

"That's interesting," he says, "I showed it to Matt last night and he said, 'Still a little slow, Dad, still a little slow.' "

To understand a culture, we study the great dramatic moments of its history, those events that get enormous attention as turning points in the life of a society: its wars, its great triumphs, its defeats, and so on. Yet, I contend that if one wants to understand a culture, it is crucial to understand moments like this one in Larry's studio.

What was it that made me experience Larry's tape as being so rapid that I had a physical reaction of hard breathing and increased heartbeat and Matt's sense that it was still "too slow"? How can two human beings respond so differently to a videotape?

Matt is Larry's twenty-three-year-old son, a member of what is often called the X Generation. His generation, born between 1961 and 1981, was raised in an electronic world. Like the Boomer Generation (born 1943–1960) and the Millennial Generation (1982-present), he grew up in an electronic culture. Those born after World War II are basically different from those of us born before that time. The technological developments since the war and innovations accompanying these developments have had profound effects on these three younger generations.

To be sure, the experiences of the three generations is different, as I shall attempt to demonstrate, but these generations have grown up in a postliterate, electronic world. It is a world very different from my own.

12

I grew up in an oral culture. While we could read and write (at least most of us), we engaged the world with proverb, story, and relationship thinking. I learned the wisdom that comes from proverbs like "Don't squat with your spurs on, buddy." Or the insight from the women of the family: "Don't let your makeup write a check your body won't cash." These proverbs were accompanied with stories told in barbershops and beauty parlors, funerals and weddings, ball games and family reunions, at truck stops and churches, on the front porch and the county-line beer joint, in your mama's kitchen and at the 13 Taxi Company.

And when we dealt with issues we addressed them in terms of their effect on our kin, our neighbors, and other relationships we had.

Then I went to college. I shall never forget the first test I took in Philosophy 101. I had prepared well. I had listed all the quotable quotes in the texts and knew the stories—all four—including one about a cave that Socrates used, albeit to me it was not very clear in its proverbial teaching. There was not a single question about even one of the "quotable quotes"—read proverbs—and the only question about a story was to ask us what the cave story "meant." Any oral person knows that the worst thing you can do is explain a story.

I didn't do too well on that test so I went to see the instructor to tell him he didn't know how to give an exam. When I got there, we got into an extended conversation in which he said to me at one point, "Tex, it's OK to read a book for its sayings and stories, but I want you to read the text for the structure of the argument."

He might as well have been talking about the other side of the moon. I had no idea what "the structure of the argument" was. I kept looking for a line drawing or a blueprint. Then he said, "Tex, if you will pay attention to the kind of verbs and nouns an author uses and the character of the modifiers of the text, you will learn to discern the basic model operative in the author's mind from which the text is written." I remember being absolutely befuddled by such arcane interests. Not only did I not understand his point I could not comprehend why anyone should want to spend their lives on such weird exploits.

That day I did not realize that I was being introduced to a literate culture that would layer on my mind a very different way of relating to the world. I was being taught to think in propositional claims, to think in theory and conceptualization, to develop ideas in linear

13

discourse. I was learning to have ideas about ideas. It was and is an extraordinary world.

At the end of college I married a beautiful woman named Peggy. For a while, it seemed, every time we looked at each other she got pregnant. Our children—two late Boomers (born 1958 and 1960) and one Xer (1963)—were quite different from us. They thought in yet other ways, neither oral nor literate. They engaged the world differently, connected with things seemingly at an oblique from the way we did. They were moved emotionally in ways we did not understand.

Partly, the cause was television. In the homes where Peggy and I were reared there was not a television set until after we had gone away to college. Our children never knew a world without TV. But it wasn't only that. Their music was not understandable, and they did things with their bodies that made me realize—to be sure, sometime later—that they were "wired with circuits" we did not have. They were and are far more like Matt than their parents. They also seem to learn differently and to approach things from another angle on life. Their memories worked in another format, and their thinking did not do analysis the way I had learned in college. They did not do critical thinking, at least the way I had been taught.

If I have been raised in an oral culture to think in proverbs, stories, and communal relationships and then educated in a literate culture to think in theory, conceptualization, and linear discourse, they engage the world through images, through sound as beat—so very evident in their music, especially rock—and through visualization. They are so decidedly other.

While this was true with our children, it is even more true of our grandchildren. The gulf between the way they engage life and the way we do is a sea. I have a granddaughter who can do her homework, watch TV, and beat me in a video game all virtually in the same half hour. I can concentrate on only one thing at a time. You say that's because I am a male. Yes, but I have a grandson who can do basically the same thing as his female cousin. It is a strange world.

I come to this work with very personal interests. I would like to understand my children and grandchildren far better than I do. I would like to get some clearer notions of what is going on with them.

Yet, it's also more than that. I want to examine what is happening in this culture, where it seems to be going and how people are being formed by it. While I cannot do a broad analysis of U.S. culture here, my hope is to characterize basic dynamics and practices of the electronic transformation we are presently going through. I want to examine the ways electronic generations think, feel, approach life, form relationships, make commitments, bond, and deal with issues of central importance. I want expressly to look at indigenous practices in electronic culture because these are basic processes of formation at work in the lives of people like my children and grandchildren.

I am also a Christian and a church person. It concerns me greatly that my children and grandchildren find church "boring" and not relevant to their lives. They are not touched by its worship services, finding them an exercise in tedium, and they find no compelling reason to commit themselves to Christ and the church. The issues I brought to the study of faith and the excitement I found in the university and the church in struggling with questions of ultimate commitment do not address the key interests of their lives. I want desperately to bridge this chasm.

It is no secret that those most influenced by electronic culture participate in church at far lower levels than those of previous generations. I believe that the failure of the church, as of yet, to deal with the changes brought on by an electronic culture is a basic factor in the lower levels of participation of post-World War II electronic generations. We face a time reminiscent of the coming of the printing press and the way in which Martin Luther, for one, addressed its implications and responded to the challenges it represented. We live in a transformation of the culture with implications even more far-reaching for the life of the contemporary church than those of Luther's time.

So I come to this work with personal, familial, cultural, and religious interests. This is no mere intellectual curiosity alone. I do not want to understand simply to understand. I want to know so that things can be changed, so that I can learn to relate to my children and grandchildren more on their terms, so that the church can find new ways to touch people's lives with what I regard as the central narrative of human life, the profoundly good news of what God has done in Christ.

I have a basic interest in how differently Matt and I saw that video. There are substantive differences between us. Neither of us will be well served if I simply decide that he is young and will "get over it." If I hide myself from his true otherness about these things electronic, I will be the poorer for it. My generation will miss out on a major transformation occurring in our lifetime. Even more important, the church could lose a key opportunity for ministry and mission. It would be tragic to live through one of the most significant transitions in the history of the world and to relegate it to a mere stage in the life of the young. We need to search these changes to discover what is happening. These events affect all our lives.

Perhaps the best place to begin such a search is by learning what it means to engage the world in images. A good many students in this field suggest that images are replacing words, that we turn increasingly to icons, not words, in communication. It would be silly to contend that images will replace words, at least in the forseeable future, but one does not have to argue that words are being eradicated to see that a real shift has occurred in the place of images in an electronic culture and to begin identifying the impact of this on the way people relate to the world.

The Formative Power of Practices

Walter Ong observes that our senses are historically and socially organized. Our senses are conditioned and influenced by the period of time in which we live and the cultures of which we are a part. This means that our sight, hearing, smell, touch, and taste are shaped by our lives as social and historical beings.[1] Constance Classen and others discuss these developments in an important book on the senses, and in a more recent study they demonstrate how much smell varies across time and cultures.[2]

Ong calls this historical and cultural organization of the senses "the sensorium." He reports that different cultures specialize in certain senses: for example, the Greeks in sight, the Hebrews in hearing, the modern West in the visual, Korea in taste, and today's electronic culture in sound.[3] Ong's life work is given over to the impact of oral, literate, and electronic forms of communication on the sensorium of people in different times and places.

Of particular interest to Ong is the significance of the coming electronic culture. He sees in this shift a major transformation in the West and the development of a radically new organization of the sensorium. To put it in the vernacular, people are being "wired" differently in the enormous changes brought by new developments in electronic technology. I shall have occasion to examine these in more detail below.[4]

Yet, there is no question that media shifts do indeed reorganize our senses and our ways of thinking. Marshall McLuhan's influential book, *Understanding Media,* first brought attention to these things on a broad scale. His famous dictum, "the medium is the message," contends that a society is influenced more by the *form of its media* than by the specific *content* of its communication, that is, "the formative power of the media are the media themselves."[5] It is "merely to say that the personal and social consequences of any medium . . . result from the new scale that is introduced into our affairs by each extension of ourselves, or by any new technology."[6]

For example, McLuhan believes that media are basically extensions of the human body.[7] That is, the wheel extends the foot; the book extends the eye; and modern media extend the central nervous system. Further, the speed of electronic communication radically changes our relation to space and time, collapsing them in such ways that we simultaneously experience events around the globe. All of these introduce a larger scale into our lives.

Hence, media create a new environment with permeating psychic and social effects. McLuhan makes a good deal of the role of classifications and analysis in literate culture, but contrasts electronic media as being more concerned with pattern recognition. Electronic media overload us with data and information with the result that the capacity to perceive configurations becomes more important than classification and connections. Illustrating his point with motion pictures he argues that the "sheer speeding up" of the "mechanical," takes us "from the world of sequence and connections into the world of creative configuration and structure. The message of the medium is that of transition from lineal connections to configurations."[8]

For example, I see a great deal of statistics on the different generations in the U.S. I cannot keep all of these data in my mind. I find it necessary to shape them into some kind of pattern or gestalt or configuration if I am to be able to "keep them with me" and use and communicate them in my consultations and lectures. This configuration will not be correct in every detail; it is therefore important that one not forget the complexity and not fail to return to it with regularity. When we construct configurations, we have to forget, but as Edgar S. Brightman used to say, we must not forget that we have forgotten.

Knowing Through Practices

The thing that strikes me most sharply in oral, literate, and electronic cultures is the differences in the practices that are basic to these three formations. For example, to move from engaging the world through proverb, story, and communal relationship to that of appropriating it through theory, conceptualization, and discourse is a move of major proportions. Today some forty-five years after first moving into college education I still find myself living in two worlds.

Sheer delight awaits when I find some book or event that puts them in juxtaposition. I have just read Matt Wray and Annalee Newitz's wonderful book, *White Trash.*[9] It is a fine piece of work in which thoughtful analyses and empathic descriptions of "disreputable" Whites are depicted in academic discourse. Yet the book has numerous stories and sayings right out of the oral culture from which most "White trash" come. Experiences like these remind me of how much I come from both worlds. To have them come together is an experience of soul.

It is my hope that I can come to participate sufficiently in practices of an electronic culture—which, of course, I do already to some extent—and that these practices will include not only the delight I find in oral and literate culture, but also help me be more in touch with the world forming around us.

It is crucial to engage in the practices of a cultural formation if one is to get some accurate sense of what goes on there. There is a knowing, both tacit and explicit, that cannot be achieved apart from the concrete, lived practices of people. I remember once reading a book on pouring cement. Not only did I read it, I outlined it. I had the ideas correctly in my mind. However, when I got a ten-inch-deep swath of wet concrete poured over a ten-by-thirty-foot area, I came to a "knowing" of cement I had not found in the book, especially since I was standing in the middle of it while wearing boots that were only eight inches high! To get in touch with a cultural formation requires that kind of involvement in the ordinary, lived practices of a form of life.

To learn a practice is to engage in a textured, sensory, kinesthetic know-how. It has to do with the skill of moves and movements. It's the development of a "touch" or the "feel" of an activity. It involves a tacit anticipation that comes with long practice: the remembering-not-to-forget. Such anticipation comes not from a checklist but from the

18

skilled habituation of a competence, the long practiced way of living in a form of life.[10]

There is an enjoyment in everyday practices well-done, the physical "high" in the satisfaction of proficiency, the ecstasy of the working or living moment, the sense of being in concert with a project, the fulfillment of working with a piece of wood, the sewing of a seam, the cooking of peas and doing it "right," the intricacies of an engine, and the nurturing touch with a distraught child. The practice of things so often ordinary are culturally and historically loaded.

Hence, understanding and engagement with a people involves the most careful attention to and participation in their indigenous practices. Not only do we learn through the indigenous practices of a people, we are also formed by practices, more so than we dream. If I stand in front of a mirror and drop my arms in a relaxed way to my sides, my right hand turns in so that the back of the hand turns toward the front. My left hand remains parallel to my left hip. The reason for this is that I spent fifteen years of my life trying to throw a baseball as hard as I could with my right arm (my fastball sometimes reached speeds of fifty miles an hour). The practice of pitching shaped my body so that now, many years later, I am physically scored by that practice.

Further, we don't realize how much we are encoded in other ways by our practices. It embarrasses me in some contexts to admit how much I like the love songs of the 1940s and 1950s: "Smoke Gets in Your Eyes," "Time on My Hands," "If I Loved You," "Till You Went Away," "People Will Say We're in Love," and many more. But those songs played at many dances and over the radio and in automobiles and on dates. I do not now merely hear them; I am encoded with responses to them. Muscle memories begin to move with that slow dancing we used to do, and sometimes I have to keep myself from swaying. They trigger old teenage feelings that surely a man of my age wouldn't have—I didn't say shouldn't—and yet there they are.

But this music also affects relationships. It is quite clear that this music is not only encoded in my spouse as well, but that it shapes our marriage. There is a romantic quality about these songs that has become part of the practices of our life together and certainly central to our practice of affection. Some people say you cannot build a marriage around romance. I say you cannot build a marriage around only romance. Romance can be a part of marriage; it depends, at least in part, on the practices that form and sustain the relationship.

19

It is also clear that the music of my grandchildren and their practices are quite different from ours. Tina Turner's song "What's Love Got to Do with It?" where she sings: "What's love but a second-hand emotion" and "who needs a heart when a heart can be broken?" is a radically different piece. While I'm sure it reflects what's going on in the culture, it must also help to encode different formations around commitment and the expression of love.

I say these things because I want to convey something of the way the various practices of oral, literate, and electronic cultures shape us, but also to underline why we are so very different and why. Quite frankly, a literate culture can often distort this very point because it is easy to come to the belief that if one "gets the ideas right" one can understand a cultural formation. I want to contest this point with the utmost urgency. We have to move beyond ideas alone to the practices of a cultural formation, which includes the practices of thinking, if we are to understand and be able to participate in this formation.

Then, why write a book? Because the people I want most to address are the people who still read them. I am especially interested in clergy and laity committed to literate culture who simply don't see what all the commotion is about with respect to electronic culture and who wonder why the church can't continue to do what it has done all along. My purpose here in this regard is to identify some of these basic practices and then encourage people to begin engaging in these, or, at least, to have the good sense to open doors to those who can do these practices and give them the permission necessary to relate the gospel to the new culture forming all around us.

The first step is to look at three basic characteristics of the practices of electronic culture in our time and in our society: engaging the world through images, sound as beat, and visualization. These will receive our attention in the following chapters.

CHAPTER TWO

Engaging the World Through Images

What does it mean to engage the world in images? In one sense, of course, there is nothing new about thinking in images. After all, print itself is visual and when we "take in" or read, we "see" images. Moreover, icons and religious art, as well as other forms of art were used long before print. But clearly this is not what is meant by image in an electronic sense. This needs closer examination. How can we understand what it means to engage the world through images in the context of an electronic culture?

Baudrillard's Semiurgic Society of Hyperreality

One answer to this question is that of Jean Baudrillard who argues that we have moved from a metallurgic society (working with metals) to a semiurgic one where increasingly we work with signs and images. He contends that the production of images and simulation creates new forms of society, culture, experience, and subjectivity. More than that, Boudrillard sees the development of hyperreality, a situation in which images are "realer than real," a setting that undermines the important distinction between reality and unreality. In fact, he believes that reality disappears altogether in this hyperreality of images and signs. The result is an "implosion of meaning" in which the great mass of people, the silent majority bored with nagging commercial advertisement and sullen with life, become impervious to meaning, messages and solicitation.

Baudrillard sees a progressive move toward unreality in semiurgic society and describes "the successive phases of the image" as follows:

—"it is the reflection of a basic reality
—it masks and perverts a basic reality
—it masks the *absence* of a basic reality
—it bears no relation to any reality whatever: it is its own pure simulacrum."[1]

Baudrillard, in essence, is saying that this kind of image is a copy without an original; that is, a purely constructed image without any actual referent.

An illustration will convey Baudrillard's point. During his presidency, Ronald Reagan argued on TV that the U.S. had a "window of vulnerability" in its defense program. This was powerful imagery and carried the day in terms of what Reagan wanted in a military budget. In fact, the country continues to struggle with a national debt because of the spending triggered by the Reagan administration to address this unprotected weakness. Yet, studies of this question have consistently found that there was no window of vulnerability. While the metaphor was a powerful image and legitimated Reagan's budgetary designs, it did not exist as a fact of military and national vulnerability.

While there is little question of the power of electronic culture to cast distorted images of things across the society, and while Reagan's "window of vulnerability" proved to be a compelling metaphor of media hyperreality, I find myself demurring at Baudrillard's semiurgic depiction. It is too absolute, and too simplistic. One must not forget how many senators and congressional representatives supported defense spending in order to gain federal money for their districts in what is without question the deepest and widest pork barrel in the history of the world. The image of a window of vulnerability may have helped legitimate the effort in Congress, but the self-interest of politicians, the potential profits of weapon makers and military suppliers, and the self-seeking of communities across the country who benefit so materially—at least in the short run—from a military-industrial complex are more basic to that astronomical inflation of defense spending than some supposed simulacra of a semiurgic society alone. Moreover, Baudrillard seems to forget at times how often fantasy gets depicted in print cultures. Rush Limbaugh, the contemporary electronic clown of hyperreality, has his literate equals.

Neil Postman's Decontextualized Imagery

Another point of view comes from Neil Postman, who argues that in an electronic culture the image replaces the word. Several serious consequences result from this shift, according to Postman.[2] First, it brings about the pseudo event and the pseudo context, "events" formed from images that have no actual referents in the world of everyday life, a position not different from Baudrillard's at this point.

Second, "knowing" becomes a "knowing about" instead of a "knowing of"; that is, one knows about the fact of hunger in, say, India, but there is no critical understanding of it in terms of an analysis of its causes or the complexities of its political and economic dynamics or the depth of the difficulty of addressing it. In this sense the "language" of imagery loses a sense of connectedness with the flow of life.

Third, electronic imagery has amnesia about the past, believing history is irrelevant, fascinating us instead with its instancy, while offering no complexity or coherence. In this sense it becomes "a decontextualized imagery."

Fourth, its specialty is performance, not ideas, and it presents an image, not an argument. For example, authentic religion is no longer possible on TV, says Postman, and the televangelist becomes the idol. In lacking consecrated space, televangelism has a bias toward secular psychology, and Postman fears that TV itself will become the content of religion. It will serve to bring personalities into our hearts rather than stimulate thought in our minds.

Fifth, Postman argues that media are the dominant influence on the formation of a culture's intelligence and social preoccupations. While media often seem innocent enough, they have powerful consequences in the "definition of reality." The introduction of a new medium in a culture transforms the practices of thinking and re-creates the content of the culture.

Postman then illustrates how the clock re-creates time, the way writing re-creates the mind, and offers an interesting account of the impact of the telegraph in the development of news as a commodity.

Finally, for now, Postman sees media as metaphors that have the capacity to influence a wide variety of attitudes and experiences; that is, media can go far beyond their immediate context to shape the culture in ways not anticipated when first introduced. He argues in this connection that "each epistemology is the epistemology of a stage of media development" (24).

Postman seems to believe that the eighteenth century was the ideal time of our national life when we were a print culture and when informed debate guided our lives. I think, however, of the fact that we were a slave society in those days and that women were clearly second-class citizens, if that. Postman knows this, of course, but because I have read some of the literate accounts supporting slavery and the demeaning characterizations of women in that world, I question his idealization of print culture and his demonizing of electronic culture in such gross terms. It is not necessary to dull oneself to the demonic in electronic culture in order to see such views as those of Postman as one-sided. It is also crucial to see the demonic in print culture. The point is that the demonic—understood in Tillich's terms as the twisting of a good—is not limited to one cultural formation.

Images in Culture and History

Obviously, talk of moving from a print culture to an image culture is abstract. It is a mistake to argue that image is replacing print for the simple reason that there is more print today than at any other time in history. For the foreseeable future print will remain a large part of the way communication is done, although electronic culture will affect the way print is carried out. The coming of the computer, the Internet, the World Wide Web, hypertext, hypermedia, virtual reality, and the explosion of technology connected with this suggest that we now have forming around us a new electronic literality. While this is not the primary focus of our attention here, it must not be missed.[3]

At the same time it would be foolish to ignore the impact of electronic culture and the significant role of images in it. For this reason I want to suggest some basic factors one needs to keep in mind in thinking about this dynamic of engaging the world in images.

The Rich Particularity of Images

The first thing to say is that there is no essence of images that will be the same in all times and places. Images, like most things, are conditioned by culture and history. People like Postman seem to suggest that there are universal characteristics that will always be in place when one thinks in images. However, if I am correct about the rich particularity of practices, one cannot come to such easy generalizations about images and their place in electronic culture. We need to look at the way they are conditioned by culture and history. We turn next to the factor of culture.

Culture and Images

"Seeing is believing" or "I'll believe it when I see it" are statements often heard in U.S. culture. It makes it sound as though believing is based on seeing. I want to argue that the exact opposite is the case, that is, we don't "see" anything until we first believe something. Even our seeing is based on basic trusts and these are learned and are endemic to culture.

Marius Von Senden conducted a study of people who had been blind their entire lives until the condition was corrected by surgery or by spontaneous remission. One might think that such persons would immediately experience a wonderful vision of the world they had never known. In fact, they could not "see" at all, or, rather, "the patient is immediately confronted with a wall of brightness containing color patches that blend indistinguishably into one another." The experience is a "swirl of color." Shapes they have known by touch, such as triangles and squares, cannot be recognized in their initial "sightedness." "The newly-operated patients do not localize their visual impressions: they do not relate them to any point, either to the eye or to any surface . . . ; they see colors much as we smell an odor . . . which enfolds and intrudes upon us, but without occupying any specific form of extension in a more exactly definable way."

These patients have no sense of visual distance and with that no notion of size. One woman, when asked "how big her mother was, . . . did not stretch out her hands, but set her two index fingers apart."

It requires hard mental effort and much learning in order to see. Otherwise, "the bright wall of sensation remains a dazzling, incoherent barrier." After surgery one young woman would close her eyes just to move around the house. The size of the world is overwhelming and with it their own insignificance. As they come to understand how visible they have been all along to others, they experience this as an invasion of their own privacy.[4]

The point here is how much effort it takes in learning to see. We easily forget how many years it took in infancy and beyond to learn to identify things in a visual field, not to mention the kind of reasoning and judgment that developed along with it. If culture can be defined as anything made and learned by humans, seeing is a major cultural achievement—a claim that requires no denial of a biological dimension for such socialization, so long as one remembers that our "biological understanding" is profoundly cultural.

The formative role of culture in seeing is also related to language. Influences here come from many directions. An interesting connection is the one Ludwig Wittgenstein formulated in mid-career when he suggested that language gives rise to images. He saw this as a cause for confusion. He argued for a more careful use of language. While his concern was with language-engendered images and the need for greater clarity about them, one does not have to believe that language gives rise to images as a one-directional move in order to acknowledge that the relations of images to language are extraordinarily complex and, of course, profoundly cultural.

Another point of cultural influence comes in the relation of images to cultural configuration or pattern. Images do not occur like some raw picture on the scene of a society but come in relation to context of a particular culture. What makes images so striking in our own time is their juxtaposition to print culture, indeed the very dependence of electronic culture on a literate one. For this reason they can seem so sharply different from the conventions of print.

Ron Burnett makes the point that images are hybrids. That is, they "are hybridized agglomerations of expression. . . . They mix with language, the visual, and oral expressions." Images are not "purely" pictorial in ordinary use, but rather are "embodied" with other forms of expressions. These, like the visual images abstractly conceived, are connected to the culture from which they arise. Burnett points out how careful analysis of images is seldom done by dealing with their "questions of meaning, comprehension, communication, and use-value."[5]

Obviously, much more could be said about images and how much they are conditioned by the culture of which they are a part. My point here is that simplistic notions of how images operate in a culture will not do. Analyses like those of Baudrillard and Postman are too narrowly conceived. Where they are correct about their capacity to distort and mislead, we, indeed, do need to be critical and wary. But to reduce the use of images to their distortive capacities is clearly to betray an unwarranted prejudice.

The Historicity of Images

Equally important in understanding electronic images in terms of culture is to see them as historically conditioned. Some writers in the field seem to suggest that images have a certain character and consequence operative in all times and places. Such views turn electronic images into ahistorical phenomena. To do so, these views not only have to ignore much of contemporary thought about the historical location of life and practice, but also fail to comprehend the changes electronic media have gone through in the short time they have been around. I see an important shift in electronic culture since World War II when TV became widely used, but one can certainly make the case that electronic culture began in the nineteenth century with the telegraph. It is needless to belabor the fact that electronic media have changed greatly since and the role of the image with them. For example, we use more images today in a tighter time frame and mix and juxtapose them in ways that were impossible just a few years ago.[6]

Furthermore, I am struck by the fact that we are in a very early period of electronic culture. Already we have seen tremendous changes in technology and undoubtedly more will come. In the century ahead the possibilities are enormous. One does not need to be naively sanguine about electronic media to see that a range of possibilities continues to open before us. To be sure, these possibilities offer many forms of threat and potential harm, but they also offer options for new futures as well, with alternatives for human flourishing. Images need not conform to the place given them by thinkers like Postman and Baudrillard, though their concern about the distorting power of images must not be ignored.

Using Images

When images are seen from this perspective, the crucial question becomes one of how they are used. Unless one believes that images have some ahistorical essence that controls us beyond our agency, our culture, and our history, then the question of their use becomes central.

Resistance to Cultural Captivity

Some thinkers believe that the culture industries of capitalism use media to dupe people into the fantasy world of commodified life. It would be foolish to deny that a good deal of such influence takes place through media. The tendency of capitalism to commodify whatever it touches is basic to its faults. As I will maintain later, the targeting of adolescents and young adults as a market and the segmenting of that market from that of older generations play a major role in U.S. lifestyles since World War II. With some regularity, we see ads like that from an automaker making the claim that their product is "not your father's Oldsmobile." While this ad seems not to have been effective—illustrating that such images are not absolute in their control—such targeting of the young in this culture has had significant impact on generational differences.

The problem, however, with arguments that see people as pawns of the culture industries is that they depict people as cultural dopes who have no capacity to resist cultural captivity or to make alternative or even opposing uses of the offerings of the media industries. Such arguments are drawing significant criticism in recent years. Janice Radway's study of the reading of romance novels by women and Ien Ang's work on women watching the soap *Dallas* focus on the uses these readers and viewers make of media products, regardless of what the cultural producers intend. While Radway and Ang have differences between them, and while neither of them is complacent about the impact of media on women, both contend that those they studied use media, at least in part, to their own ends. A 1994 study by Tricia Rose on hip-hop and rap music demonstrates how young African Americans in the cities of the nation take the products of the culture industries and put them to their own uses in alternative and oppositional ways.[7] Finally, recent research indicates that Generation X and Millenial youth are "media sophisticates" and "astute observers of mass media."[8]

Use of Image As a Practice

One more aspect of the use of image needs to be addressed, and that has to do with the particularity of image use in a practice. It is easy to take a few categories about image, give them some kind of universal cast in terms of how images operate, and then imperialistically impose them on a large variety of settings. I oppose this procedure as sharply as I can.

The use of an image needs "thick description" in Clifford Geertz's terms.[9] As Geertz says, this involves "descending into detail." An example can help here. My granddaughter, who is fourteen, and I recently got into a discussion about a rock group she likes and a particular piece she likes to dance to. I don't like the song or the group because I find them misogynist and, frankly, a paradigm of adolescent posturing though they are all in their twenties. I did not, however, say this to my granddaughter. I had done my homework and had bought the sheet music because I could not understand the words as they sang them on the video. I observed to my granddaughter that she seemed to like that particular song and the artists—I almost gagged when I called them "artists." She admitted that she did. I started slowly.

"Well, honey, what do they say in the song? I have difficulty understanding the words on the video." I tried to couch my language so that I was not lying. I *do* have trouble understanding the words as sung, although I had the lyrics in my back pocket.

"I don't know, Grandpa, I never listen to the words."

"What do you mean you don't listen to the words?"

"Well, I just don't listen to it for that, I mean . . . , I hear them, but I just don't pay attention to them."

Rather, she likes the way the group looks and and the way they move and dance. In terms of the words, she likes the way they sound—that is, the percussive beat of the words. She especially likes to dance to the piece, especially when the video is projected on a big screen.

Notice the use each of us makes of that video. I focus on its discourse and the woman-hating character of its lyrics. Visually, I am not enamored with the dress of the group or their hairstyles, and their dance moves are not those encoded in my muscular-skeletal structure—so much for my visual appropriation of it. My granddaughter, who does not appreciate negative views of women, does not even know what the words say. (I realize that some youth won't acknowledge that they know the lyrics even when they do, but in this case I have reason to believe she is honest with me.) Her use of the video focuses on the visual dimensions of it and, of course, its beat, which we will take up shortly, but she is not listening for its discursive "message."

This is but one very simple case of the differences in use of visual images and percussive sounds by her, on the one hand, and of my more literate focus on the semantics of the lyrics while actually attempting to ignore the visual display that captured her attention, on the other. But such "simple cases" abound in our society and populate the uses of images, videos, and electronic media more generally. My point is that thick description of images must take into account their quite different uses by people if our work is to have interpretive power.

The Capacities of Images

So much has been made of the negative consequences of images that their promise is often neglected. We fail to see how the use of images can open up new ways of engaging the world and new approaches to a host of issues and problems.

The work of Larry Smarr at the University of Illinois is especially significant at this point. He finds that our minds take in images much more rapidly than they do print. Smarr's work focuses on the difference in the capacity of the brain's mental "text computer" and the eye-brain system's capacity to take in images. Our "text computer" is our brain's capacity to read print on a page. Smarr discovers that this text computer can take in print at a rate of one hundred bits per second, but the eye-brain system can take in a billion bits per second.[10] I am intrigued by the potential this offers in terms of taking on problems we've not yet been able to solve. To be sure, we have not yet adequately tapped into the resources such capacities can open up, and I don't mean only virtual reality as significant as that is, but rather the ways in which thinking can address problems from different angles and, one hopes, in effective ways. Joshua Meyrowitz states, "It is possible that video and computer games are introducing our children to a different way of thinking that involves the integration of multiple variables and overlapping lines of simultaneous actions."[11] We are only at the beginning of electronic culture.

We have another granddaughter who is diagnosed as "developmentally delayed." Her young life has been a difficult struggle because of serious learning disabilities. While she is, of course, an absolutely adorable child as all grandchildren are, she is also this beaming, photogenic rush of enthusiasm. She loves music and moves to a beat and can brighten a room just by walking into it. And she comes up with one-liners that will simply knock you off your chair. Yet for all her charisma, she is trapped in a host of disabilities. When she was ten years old, she still could not write or print her name. Despite her work in special education for all of her four years in grade school, she simply had not been able to learn to do so. Shortly after her tenth birthday her mother brought home a computer, the only one they had ever had. The *first* time Hailey sat down at the computer keyboard, she typed out her name on the screen!

Six months later her mother bought a computer program that had a procedure for making greeting cards. In a very short time Hailey became quite proficient at making greeting cards of such quality that I want her to make mine for Christmas. One evening I asked her to show me how she did it.

"Well, Grandpa, you push this [the mouse] so that that thing [the cursor] goes over to this picture [icon on the screen] and push this [button on the mouse]." Then she went through a series of steps with the mouse moving from one icon to another and in a short time had a greeting card coming out of the printer.

I said, "Wow, Hailey, your grandpa can't do that!"

"That's your problem, Grandpa," she said as a matter of fact and with no little cogency. I reflect often on her comment not only as it applies to me, but also about how it applies to the church and its recalcitrant unwillingness to take electronic culture seriously. Again, this is no reason to forget the enormous capacity of electronic culture for harm, but I wonder at the same time what possibilities it offers for people caught in a host of traps not unlike those of Hailey.

Contemporary Characteristics of Images

Having said these things about engaging the world through images, are there some characteristics of images as they are currently used in this culture that are helpful to know in terms of their implications for understanding different generations and for the church?

Wade Clark Roof makes use of Postman's work on the impact of electronic media on the religion and spirituality of the Boomer generation. While learning from Postman, his claims are more circumspect and avoid the one-sidedness of Postman and Baudrillard. Roof suggests that the shift from being a print culture to becoming an electronic one has had an important effect on Boomers. He argues that the Boomer generation is heavily influenced by a "visual mode of communication" in the way they think about salvation because of a shift from the printed word to image.[12]

He agrees with Postman that television is the culmination of a history of electronic culture that began "with photography and film in media epistemologies from a print culture" that then moved "to a culture of decontextualized imagery." While Roof acknowledges that "hard evidence" is not available to support this shift, there is, nevertheless, "a close affinity" between electronic modes of communication and Boomer "religious and spiritual styles."[13]

Again following Postman, he states that in a print culture priority is "given to the objective, to the rational use of the mind." This fosters "religious discourse with logically ordered content." Such a culture leads to a flourishing of "doctrinal debate and theological reflection."[14] This approach to religion is certainly more characteristic of my generation and of myself. I remember when I began to get seriously into the study of philosophy how important it was to attempt to hammer out a more "rational" and defensible position on matters theological.

While I now have major reservations about how "objective" any point of view is, and some time ago gave up on finding an Archimedean point from which I or anyone else could look upon life and faith with a disinterested and impartial perspective, I still find myself coming at things quite differently than most of the Boomer and Xer students I now teach.

Roof is closer to their approaches when he suggests that in an electronic culture, where images are prominent, the subjective is more important than the objective with the result that "the constant flow of ever-changing images replaces the coherent, orderly arrangement of ideas."[15] This "fluidity and instantaneity" not only shapes what we know, but shifts the process of knowing itself.

I started teaching about the time the Boomers entered theological education. I began to hear for the first time, at least on that scale, the use of the phrase "true for me." It was strange language. Peter Bertocci, Bordon Parker Bowne Professor of Philosophy at Boston University, used to say to us that when making a truth claim one does not say "true for me." You either make a truth claim or you don't. If it is true, it is true for all. "True for me" is an instance of special pleading and has no place in truth claims, he taught us. I find it very difficult to impress this teaching on Boomers and I don't mean only when addressing a question that is specific to an individual: I mean even when they address questions that involve major concerns like social theory or theology. I regard this difficulty as a shift from a more "objective" approach to more "subjective" ones.

Roof goes on to say that the use of fast-moving images reconstructs our "sense of reality" as itself in constant change, "without permanence," and we are transferred "from one psychological world to another—not unlike the images, insights, thoughts, and emotions that arise out of the inner life of the spiritual pilgrim." Roof sees this shift from the world of print to that of image as one reason why "psychological imagery is so widespread."[16]

I think here of the place that the metaphor of "journey" has come to have among Boomers and Xers. In my work in a theological school and in speaking across the United States I find a pervasive interest in "journey spirituality." These uses of "journey" reflect the role of images on "the inner life of the spiritual pilgrim." Moreover, I often find this journey spirituality populated with psychological language and often no little psychobabble.

It is not Roof's point, and certainly not mine, that images are a one-factor theory for explaining these shifts that have taken place, but rather a reflection, in part, of the impact of electronic culture and of image as important aspects of that.

Images do not usually occur in a highly abstract form as used in electronic culture. They are typically an aspect of a more fully orbed use that may involve many of the senses, especially sound and music. We move to the important ways in which sound, especially music, have affected the generations born after World War II. This will engage us in the next chapter.

CHAPTER THREE

Sound As Beat

I am a visiting preacher in a church out west. In the service of worship we are down to the time for the anthem, which comes right before I preach. The director gets up to go to the front of the choir. As she does, the pastor leans over to me and says, "We are very excited about our new choir director. She is highly trained, knows a great deal about church music, relates well to contemporary expressions, and has a wonderful charisma about her."

She steps up on a platform that is a three-quarter-inch piece of plywood covered with a plush carpet (or so I surmise), and the platform becomes something of a drum for her high-heeled shoes when she begins to direct. Her interpretation of "A Mighty Fortress Is Our God" has a powerful beat so that she not only punches the air with her hands but she also pounds the platform with her two-and-a-half-inch-heeled shoes. She belts out each beat like a professional fighter who knows how to close out a match.

She is a younger Boomer and beat is obviously deeply encoded in her being and style. Wade Clark Roof observes that music sensitized the Boomers to "the auditory dimensions of experience."[1] I don't know when I have seen such a sharp illustration of his point. She not only feels it, she embodies it.

There *is* one problem with this scene. The choir is my age. While she pounds the air and the platform, and her whole body vibrates with beat, the choir is singing a morbid adagio. The anthem, as sung, has all the pulsating power of a humming refrigerator. I think of the sailor on an aircraft carrier who gives the dramatic gestures for planes to take off, only I envision the airplanes as kites, slowly ascending as on a tether. She looks like a whirling dervish amidst a people prostrate in prayer who quietly fell asleep. I sit there asking myself: How long can she last?

This image of that day occurs to me often as I think about the different ways that the generations are encoded with sound and the implications this form of acculturation has for the society and the church. It runs deep. And it is a lot more than beat in some abstract sense. To be sure, all of my generation is not as deadly as that choir, and we can appreciate a beat in music, but the difference is substantive.

Chukwulozie Anyanwu in his study of traditional Africa says that sound is the model of reality and the criterion of truth in that culture.[2] To put it too simply, if something doesn't sound "right," it will not be true or real or authentic. While I certainly do not equate the way sound is used in traditional Africa and the way it is used by younger generations in the U.S., Anyanwu's comment triggers a way to think about the shifting place of sound as beat in our cultural context.

In the West, knowledge typically has a visual metaphor. For example, we say the following: "I see what you mean." "From my perspective." "Do you see what I mean?" "On my point of view." We use a host of these in the ways we describe knowing and understanding. Martin Jay argues that there is a "scopic regime" in the West, that is, "a singular and determining 'way of seeing.' "[3] Chris Jenks marshals evidence that "the dramatic confluence of an empirical philosophical tradition, a realist aesthetic, a positivist attitude towards knowledge and a technoscientistic ideology through modernity have led to a common-sense cultural attitude of literal depiction in relation to vision."[4]

But these influences are of a more technical and theoretical kind. If you will but think of the array of expressions we use everyday to talk about knowing and how visual they are metaphorically, you can see how pervasive this influence is.

Yet, the electronic organization of the senses involves a change in this "scopic regime." I think of how important the phrases, "I hear you saying" or "I hear you": have become with Boomers in the past few decades. These responses have been around before, certainly, but they have taken on a different shape with Boomers and participate in a larger shift. It is a subtle but obvious shift.

It is not subtle when one looks at the role of popular culture and especially, as we shall see, the place of rock music and its decided impact on the growing importance of sound, and especially sound as beat.

So far I mention only Boomers, not because they are the only generation to have gone through this shift, but because they are the first. But sound as beat has taken on major importance for the generations born since World War II. In fact, this shift, now going on for more than fifty years, has taken new directions. If Boomers are deeply influenced by TV and rock music, the X Generation and the Millennials are additionally shaped by the coming of the personal computer and the emerging development of digitalization and their resulting visualization.

Two rather common examples illustrate the ongoing importance of sound as beat. One concerns a quaint shopping center in a large midwestern city of about a million and a half people. The shopping center has a traditional "feel" about it. It has artificial gaslights, small shops, awnings in front of many businesses, a variety of ethnic eating establishments, narrow sidewalks, small streets, and boutiques that appeal to an adult clientele. It is a bit like walking back into small-town America.

Then the teenagers of this city "discover" it! It becomes the "in place" to be, and they begin to gather there every weekend beginning on Friday afternoon. They jam the place, crowd the stores, fill up the sidewalks, and make the small narrow streets little more than moving parking lots with their continual circling through the area. Meanwhile, the teens are financially wrecking the merchants with all this attention. The young people look, but don't buy. It's not their kind of "stuff." Adults won't come because it takes too long to get in to the area, to find a parking place, and then to work their way through the crowds.

The merchants know they have to do something to survive. They don't want to do anything illegal, and they don't want to be mean to the young people because they want them to be customers someday. Finally, someone comes up with the idea of playing "easy listening music." When they do the young people leave. Sound can bring the spirit or it can drive the spirit away. Easy listening music is not their "soul music." Following a cue from Anyanwu it is not "true," it is not "real," and it is not authentic. This story is a parable for those churches that will not bother to learn and practice the soul musics of the great majority of people in this culture.

The second event is equally devastating in terms of the mission of the church. A midwestern shopping mall becomes a gathering place for homeless people. During the wintertime its warmth and inviting sitting areas are very attractive to the homeless, especially when they must leave shelters in the early morning. The merchants of the shopping area do not like and do not want these "disreputable people" in the mall.

They are finally able to make them leave when they start playing Bach. These homeless people prefer the cold of winter to the genius of Bach. Such is the power of sound to draw and to repel. I often think in this connection of the church as the church of the poor and the ways in which our tastes in music and a host of other things keep us from the very people so prominently prized in Scripture.

But it illustrates how important sound as beat is in contemporary society. Two authorities from electronic culture speak to this issue. The first is Mickey Hart, one of the drummers of the Grateful Dead, who says, "the universe is . . . rhythm."[5] Or consider the teen who re-phrased Descartes's famous line, "I think, therefore I am," with a more culturally pregnant claim of her own: "I vibrate, therefore I am!" To lay out what this means we need to look at a short "history" of popular music in the last half of this century.

A Discourse on "Moving Your Tail"

Larry Hollon and I teach a course we call "White Soul." In it we work with the sociology of working people and country music. We attempt to understand the lives of rural and urban White working people in the United States and the ways that much of country music reflects their lived lives. It's a week-long course that meets four hours a day for five days. One of the requirements of the course is that our students spend at least two nights that week in a "cultural center" where working people gather and where country music is played live. These cultural centers are sometimes called "honky tonks."

Peggy and I always go, and these places usually have dance floors. When the band plays one of those slow ballads, known as a "belly rubber" or a "buckle polisher," we get up to dance. I boast that no student at our school has ever done slow dancing as well as we do. (Dizzy Dean used to say that if you have a fastball it ain't bragging.) Well, we ought to be good, we've been doing this stuff for over forty years, and we've got it down pat. We breathe in, we turn left; we breathe out, we turn right. If one of us coughs, we spin.

But then they play one of those rockabilly songs, the ones with the fast beat. Peggy and I are like a lot of churches. We do what we've always done: we do a version of the 1950s bop. So we do a downbeat version where we basically emphasize the first and third beat of the music.

When we go back to our seats, one of our students will inevitably say, "Sample, you can't dance." They never say it to Peggy, only to me. I say, "I think I just did." They say, "No, you can't dance." When I press them, they say, "You can't move your tail." I say, "That's because I graduated from high school the year Hank Williams died," which always gets a confused look from the student. If they pursue the question, I assign them 750 pages of reading in order to understand my comment. If you want to do "violence" to Generation X electronic students, give them 750 pages of reading to understand why their professor cannot move his posterior. It is absolutely delicious generational revenge!

Without going into all the details of that history, let me do an abbreviated version to whet your appetite. If you have further interest you can find in the notes of this chapter more than 750 pages to support the version recorded here in the text.

Hank Williams died in the backseat of his Cadillac during the early morning of January 1, 1953. He was on his way to a gig in Canton, Ohio. In his memory our Brookhaven High School Class of '53 made his great hit "Your Cheatin' Heart" our class theme song, which we sang with camp gusto at every class party and after the formal graduation exercises.[6]

The summer after his death another young man, eighteen years old, went to Sun Records in Memphis to do a record. Marion Keisker, a partner with Sam Phillips, met this shy teenager "with the long, greasy, dirty-blond hair." The young man would later say that he went there to make a record for his mother or to see what he sounded like, but he was there to be "discovered." Nothing happened that first visit except that Phillips and Keisker noted that the boy had an interesting voice with ballads.

The young man continued to drop by through the summer and fall, asking with increasing insecurity whether any band needed a singer. But it would not be until the next summer that Phillips and Keisker would invite him down for another session. That session and some others didn't work either, but one day while working with Scotty

Moore and Bill Black, he began to play around with an old blues song by Arthur "Big Boy" Crudup, "That's All Right [Mama]." Treating it with a rock and roll style and with Bill Black providing the combination of a slap beat and a tonal beat at the same time and with Scotty Moore continuing to simplify his work on guitar, the piece began to take on a chemistry. The young singer became increasingly confident and his singing took on a loose and freed up quality. Later they would add an old bluegrass song, "Blue Moon of Kentucky," but with a rock and roll beat to the back side, and they had a hit.[7]

This was the beginning of stardom for Elvis Presley and four years later, in 1958, when he entered the army, he was known all over the world. The year 1954 was an important year for rock and roll. For example, it was in 1954 that The Chords hit the charts for their song "Sh Boom! Sh Boom!" They were the first African American group to go to the top of the charts in the country.

After his tour of duty in the army Elvis went to Hollywood and made all those bad movies. He said *King Creole* was the exception. While he had been consumed with making movies, significant events had occurred in rock. The Beatles came on the scene and rocked the youth market, before breaking up in 1970. Other bands, like the Rolling Stones, joined the invasion of British groups coming to the U.S.

By 1968 it had been almost ten years since Elvis had been in front of a live audience. He was afraid that he no longer "had it." With some apprehension he decided to do a major television special both to determine his place on the new scene and to move back into concerts and a broader presence in the media.

In the years that Elvis made films one other critical music event occurred. Back up to 1958. Note that Elvis's "That's All Right" and "Blue Moon of Kentucky"—in fact, all of his rock and roll music prior to 1965—are "downbeat." That is, the emphasis is on the first and third beat of a four/four rock and roll song. Sing "That's All Right" and you will hear the accent come on the down beat:

That's all *rii* ight *Maa* ma. *That's* all *right* for *you*."

It is sung "*Boom* dah, *Boom* dah, *Boom* dah, *Boom* dah, *Boom* dah."

This is the way we sang music up until the mid-1960s.

Another example from the big band era. One of my favorite tunes was "In the Mood." Listen to the beat:

"*Dah* duh *dah* duh *dah* duh *dah* duh *dah* duh duh *daah*!"

Notice that it is all downbeat until the very last two notes, in which the accent is changed to upbeat. When you hear the classical rendition of it by Glenn Miller and his orchestra, you will notice that the whole band plays only one upbeat note and that at the very end of the phrase. I think it's because they don't want you to think they made a mistake!

Something very important happened in the mid-1960s that radically changed popular music. We even know the date, a conversion event, if you will. On May 12, 1965, a group of musicians were working in a studio when Jerry Wexler, a producer, made a suggestion to them. He said, "Why don't you pick up on this thing here?" He then demonstrated what he meant by doing a brief dance step. Guitarist Steve Cropper, who was there, later reported:

> [Wexler] said this was the way the kids were dancing; they were putting the accent on two. Basically, we'd been one-beat-accenters with an after beat, it was like "boom dah," but here this was a thing that went "un-chaw," just the reverse as far as the accent goes. The backbeat was somewhat delayed, and it just put it in that rhythm and [drummer] Al [Jackson] and I have been using that as a natural thing now, ever since we did it. We play a downbeat and then two is almost on but a little bit behind, only with a complete impact. It turned out to be a heck of a thing.[8]

The tune that grew out of this session is Wilson Pickett's "In the Midnight Hour," a crossover hit. Susan McClary points out that this song "gave rise to a new style of soul," and, very important, a new way of "experiencing the body." It emerged as part of "a widely shared vocabulary of physical gestures and expressions into the culture."

Cropper's comment that this new beat became "a natural thing" for him indicates how something that is socially constructed seems so "natural," says McClary. She points out how clearly it demonstrates that "musical grooves" have a history and so does the body. This event points to the mutual influence of "physical gestures and musical imagery." In this case the band grabbed onto a dance step being used by African American kids, put it through a musical interpretation, and sent it across the country through the music industry to a wide range of youth and young adults who in turn responded to it with enormous enthusiasm. McClary observes: "Music depends on our experiences as embodied beings for its constructions and its impact; but our experiences of our own bodies—our repository of proper or even possible motions and their meanings—are themselves often constituted (to a much greater extent than we usually realize) through musical imagery."[9]

When people dance to "In the Midnight Hour" they do indeed pick up on Jerry Wexler's "this thing here" dance step, and they translate the microsecond delay in that "un *chaw*" into rhythmic moves that emphasize the butt, a set of gestures known as the Jerk.[10] I never learned the Jerk. It is basic to my inability to "move my tail," and our younger students recognize it without fail.

Click back to Elvis and the 1968 television special. In this special we find a "textbook case" of the downbeat/upbeat dynamic reported by Wexler. Apparently Elvis wants to be as close to his audience as he can be, hoping to be as attuned with them as possible. He is on a small stage in the middle of the audience. It is rectangular and only about waist-high off the floor with the front row of the audience sitting around the stage with their elbows resting on it.

Early in the show Elvis does "That's All Right." As he sings, everyone in the audience is right with him clapping on the downbeat. It is, of course, a rousing piece. It is "Boom dah" all the way. Some ten or fifteen minutes later he does "Jailhouse Rock." I am told by Robert W. "Bob" Winstead, from Atlanta, now a pastor but a former professional drummer, that you simply cannot play "Jailhouse Rock" on the downbeat.[11] When Elvis starts to sing, a very interesting pattern of rhythmic clapping with the song begins in the studio. As the camera pans the audience, you can see that the first three rows—very young Boomers in their early to mid-twenties—are clapping to the song on the upbeat. They have this "un chaw" down pat, or *up* pat as the case may be. But look at the fourth row, an older group—my generation!—continues to clap on the *down*beat. *They clap on the downbeat virtually throughout the entire song.* The one exception occurs at the very end of the rendition when Elvis begins to pound out the upbeat with his right hand, perhaps trying to get my age-group on board. It requires the explicit direction of Elvis himself, it seems, to get my generation on the upbeat. No wonder that I cannot move my tail![12]

Read accounts of Elvis's early career. He was often accused of making obscene moves when he first started out, a charge he consistently denied. He often said he did not do "dirty moves." He argued that he only did leg moves, meaning not pelvic ones. When you look back at his early concerts and TV appearances, he's correct. I suspect that whatever his own personal commitments here, his early career preceded the shift to upbeat rhythm and the resultant pelvic gestures.

Our senses, our feelings, our bodies, and our ways of engaging life are culturally and historically structured. We do not have some singular human nature that is the same in all times and places, but rather we are in great part made up of the practices, the relations, the forms of life and the times of which we are a part. I really am "wired differently" from my children and grandchildren. What speaks to me does not speak to them. What moves me, entertains me, touches me is not what does so to them. People of my age will not engage younger generations until we recognize this otherness, and concede that along with images, sound and especially sound as beat are crucial to that recognition.

The Larger Cultural and Historical Context

Of course, I am not attempting to account for all of the history of popular culture and the shifts in popular music in the story above. But it does illustrate the symbolic importance of sound as beat to these younger generations and, further, how seemingly small shifts can reveal more significant changes in experience and perception. I see this story in some sense as a parable, one pregnant with the import of sound as beat in cultural practices since World War II. It is part of a list of cultural practices that gives some sense of the larger context.

Economically, it is important to see capitalism in historical perspective. Earnest Mandel, an economic historian, places the history of capitalism into three periods: 1840–1890, competitive capitalism; 1891–1940, monopoly capitalism; and 1941 to the present, late or consumerist capitalism.

The first stage of capitalism brought a technological revolution of steam and iron, and railways and print media introduced new forms of distribution, transportation, and consumption. In this stage the concentration was on production. With respect to youth and young adults, this was the Victorian period with its strict and repressive forms of nurture.

The second stage built upon developments of electricity and steel and of electric and combustion engines. Automobiles and radios became the possession of virtually every household. The idea of adolescence emerged in the thirty years from 1890–1920. It was the inchoate step of a new form of generational difference.

In the third, or consumerist, stage of capitalism we saw the coming of electronics and automation. Air travel, television, and recent rapid technological developments made central impacts. Furthermore, after World War II the United States became the dominant power on the globe; it stood alone among the major industrial powers of the world with its industry at full operating power since it did not suffer the destruction of other nations. Profits increased greatly in post-war America and the average family income almost doubled in the twenty- to twenty-five-year period after 1945.[13] Large numbers of young adults, married women, and racial ethnics entered the workforce and became a market for consumer goods. With this came competitive pressures to increase the rate of technological innovation both to stimulate and to meet this growing demand. These economic fortunes released a major market for consumer goods.

This international, national, economic, cultural, commercial, consumerist framework provides the context for the emergence of an electronic culture as it takes form in the late-twentieth century. Accompanying these events is a leap in the entertainment industry, in motion pictures, recording and playback equipment, and later in computers, digitalization, and virtual reality. While popular culture and entertainment are a "result" of these shifts, they are also a major stimulus to these changes because they so markedly enhance consumption. They do not simply mirror the transformations but play a basic role in them.[14]

The lifestyle impact of these changes must not be missed either. After World War II marketers discovered that youth and young adults buy most of the movie tickets and music records. At that point a fateful effort was made to target the young as a specific and segmented market. This means not only finding what would sell, but also convincing young Americans that they are different from their parents and other older Americans. The Boomers are the first generation to experience this on such an enormous scale. Notions about the "New Generation" are directly affected by such target marketing and segmentation. It is probably not possible to measure the impact of such efforts in the development of generational identity, conflict, differences, and tensions that continue with the Xers and, as we shall see in the near future, the Millennialists.

Click back to sound as beat, but don't visualize beat as a reductionist theory, but rather as a parable of the times. First, Elvis cannot be understood as a phenomenon of the 1950s apart from the fact that a host of music producers had already seen what a rich lode of music and musical talent resided in the African American tradition, and there were tremendous market pressures to come up with new "products." But how could they get White Americans to buy it? They needed a medium, a voice, a talent who could make that transition. Elvis could sing a blues form of country music and make even bluegrass records "rock and roll." He was, of course, an extraordinary talent in and of himself. He was electric with the young. But he also served as a breakthrough, a means to new musical formations. While there were other artists like Carl Perkins, Johnny Cash, Bill Haley, Little Richard, Buddy Holly and others who should not be forgotten in this transition, no one was more important, even *as* important, as Elvis in opening that door.

In response to the new music, innovations from this emerged in dancing. It is no idle happenstance that Jerry Wexler drew on the dance steps he saw among Black youth and the "un chaw" upbeat developed. This is an example of the convergence of a social construction in formation. It also points to the fact that we make a mistake if we think human beings are but flotsam on some huge cultural and historical river of social predestination. Such accounts require obliteration of human agency and the consignment of real people to the role of cultural dopes.

Certainly, we are powerfully influenced by these mammoth movements afoot in our lives. Culture and history are imputed into our very everyday being. Muscle and bone are socially formed, not only by diet and exercise—as cultural and historical as they are—but by the concrete practices and relationships that create the "atmosphere" of "the worlds" in which we live and move and have our being. And for fifty years now "sound as beat" has played exactly such a role in forming the generations of those years.

Still, we continue to be historical beings. No formation is permanent. Already new shifts are taking place. Our senses vary not only across time and formations, but in relationship to one another. Such a shift seems to be forming before our very eyes and ears. For lack of a better word, I will call it "visualization." New social constructions are coming into place. The ratio of the senses is changing. If one can argue that there is a hierarchy of the senses, meaning that one of the senses or more takes on significantly more salience in one culture or another or in one time more than another, we seem to be in such a time. We turn to this next.

CHAPTER FOUR

The Visual as Visualization

Nobody in the history of baseball stole more bases in his lifetime than Ty Cobb (892), and nobody ever would . . . at least until Lou Brock came along. By the mid-1960s Maury Wills was the premier base stealer in baseball, the standard by which all such thievery was judged. Wills kept a little black book in which he made notes on all the idiosyncrasies of the league's pitchers when they had a runner from the opposing team on base. He took note of tip-offs, little twitches, telltale signs, anything a pitcher did that would give him that fraction of a second, those extra feet or even inches that would allow him to get back to first on a pickoff attempt by the pitcher or to get to second ahead of the catcher's throw.

Beginning in 1964 Lou Brock got an eight-millimeter camera and took movies of the pitchers in the league. These films were quite helpful. In 1965 he stole sixty-three bases, and by 1974 he began stealing a hundred or more a year, which he then did eight of the next nine years, leading the league, and eventually totaling a lifetime mark of 938, and, of course, breaking Cobb's record. "If Wills had his black book, Brock thought, I've got my camera—I'm a man of modern technology."[1]

The Shift to Visualization

It does not take anything away from Brock's extraordinary athletic talent and competitive desire to say that he also represents a basic and important shift taking place in the larger culture. Technological developments, consumer trends, and the increasing role of film and then videotape are aspects of a significant move toward visualization in everyday life. If Wills's notebook represents writing and print culture,

Brock's camera depicts that of electronic culture and the growing significance of visualization.

In using the word *visualization* I want to suggest something different than visuality in its most general sense. I aim to focus on the practices dealing explicitly with the screen in electronic culture. That is, the coming of electronic culture and the screen introduce an entire range of practices not previously present to the world. At the same time visualization affects life in more ways than those activities of being immediately in front of a screen. The impact of visualization cannot be reduced to viewing alone. Further, visualization must not be conceived abstractly, but seen as it occurs in contexts where a great deal more is going on than visualization alone. As we shall see below, visualization takes on even greater force when combined with percussive images and sound as beat. Finally, it is important to see that practices taking shape around visualization bring on new kinds of encoding or "wiring." We are being reconstructed as human beings by the coming of visualization.

The coming of motion pictures on a large public scale began in the 1920s, and the American people became avid movie fans long before the post-World War II period, and TV moved this to a new level. Today the ever-increasing computer technology as well as video and now virtual reality and digitalization are taking us to yet newer formations of visualization as the technology becomes more affordable or "democratic."

The Changing Ratio of Sound and Visualization

The impact of visualization can be seen as well in the development of popular music, especially rock and its aftermath. Lawrence Grossberg, in a very important discussion of the contemporary situation that we will consider later, traces the history of "the rock formation." By "rock" he means the "entire range of postwar, 'youth'-oriented, technologically and economically mediated, musical practices and styles." By "formation" he understands that musical practices are always located "in the context of a complex (and always specific) set of relations with other cultural and social practices."[2] Hence when addressing the "rock formation" he means a cultural formation rather than a only a musical one.

Grossberg points out that the Boomers, as a very large population cohort growing up in the socioeconomic context of postwar America, developed a certain relation to sound—an aspect of the sensorium in Ong's terms—which was clearly affected by the technological developments in music and the practices associated with them: "Technological developments changed musical practices at every point in the cycle of production: amplification in performance; magnetic tape in recording (allowing sophisticated intervention between production and recording); and transistorization in consumer reception."[3] These developments make possible a growing "sophisticated manipulation" in the use of sound and music.

However, a different set of circumstances in the socioeconomic context, the music industry, the financial well-being of different generational groups, and a changing technology has had a significant effect in terms of our focus here. If the Boomers were influenced by sound and especially sound as beat, Grossberg, writing in the early nineties, observes that *"the ratio of sight and sound has already changed significantly."*[4] He argues that *the visual* in MTV, films for youth, and even network TV has *"for the first time since the early 1960s, successfully constructed a youth audience . . . [and is] displacing sound* as the locus of generational identification, differentiation, investment and occasionally even authenticity."[5]

There is an abundance of anecdotal evidence to support Grossberg's claim. A ten-year-old gets off a subway in New York City and asks a friend: "Have you *seen* the latest Michael Jackson song?"[6] Some now maintain that we should no longer call teenagers by that name but "screenagers" instead. Many of us wait for our grandchildren to visit in order for them to set the clock on our VCR, to get the date correct on our fax machine, to teach us new ways to use our computer, and to discover additional resources on the Internet and World Wide Web. It is not lost on me that my grandchildren understand their screen-agility as a significant means for differentiating their generation not only from their Silent Generation grandparents but from their Boomer parents as well.

But the evidence goes well beyond the anecdotal, according to recent studies, and consistent findings come out between those born before World War II and those born after. First, a marked difference appears in reading practices. One survey reports that "the percentage of 18 to 24 year olds who read novels, short stories, poetry, and plays in the previous year" dropped 7% between 1982 (60%) and 1992 (53%) [26]. Yet, this practice declined only 2% among middle-aged adults or Boomers, but remained stable with adults 50 years old or more. Among young adults 41% "did not read a single book not required for school or work in the last twelve months, and 60% read four or less" [26].

At the same time, visual activities increase in participation. Among 18 to 24 year olds, 29% report visits to art museums or galleries in 1992 compared to 23% in 1982, and TV and video dealing with art are up from 18% to 26% in these same years [26]. This increase is all the more interesting since formal arts education in school is down from 41% to 24% in this ten-year period [27].

The impact of TV on both Boomers and young adults can be found in their viewing patterns in relation to older generations. The real difference is not between Boomers and young adults, but rather between them and older adults, fifty years of age and more. Young adults watch TV three hours a day, consistent with viewing practices of previous generations when they were their age. These young adults are more likely to watch the top-rated shows than MTV while the fifty-plus-year-olds watch "60 Minutes" and "Murder She Wrote" [27].

Going to the movies is down for young adults from 87% a decade before the study to 82% in 1992. Yet, this still stands in sharp contrast to the 59% among adults of all ages [28].[7] This decline among these young adults is a reflection of their deteriorating economic condition, on the one hand, and on the other hand their increasing use of the computer, the VCR, the Internet/World Wide Web, and so forth. The two factors may also be related to each other.

Just as the use of video by Lou Brock changed the way one studied base stealing or any opponent in sports, so has the use of the screen changed a great many practices in the larger culture, not the least of which is the impact of visualization on popular music.

The Reality of Visual Argument

The coming of visualization also seems to affect not only the ways younger people engage the world but also the ways in which they make judgments about what is convincing and true and how reality is perceived. Howard Snyder reports on an article in the *Scientific*

American that discusses contemporary trends in mathematics. With increased use of computers, computer graphics, and screens, an interesting shift seems to be occurring with math students.

Mathematicians working with high school teachers argued that proofs were essential in teaching math to make sure that a given computation is correct. But this drew serious question from these teachers because they found such forms of proof not nearly as convincing as, for example, visual arguments. The great majority of these high school teachers contended that their students do not relate to or find important the traditional ways of arriving at "proof" in the discipline of mathematics.

Snyder calls attention to the implication here:

> Visual reality has become more real, and thus more convincing, than rational argument or mathematical proof. This signals a turning point in cultural perception. Perhaps it means that increasingly a person's or group's worldview will be literally that, a world*view,* not a set of arguments or ideas or concepts. Here is an example of postmodern perception. Yet in some ways it is closer to premodern and "primitive" perceptions than to modern ones.[8]

By "premodern" and "primitive" perceptions, Snyder seems to be contrasting modern and print culture—with its emphasis on arguments, ideas, and concepts—on the one hand, with premodern and oral culture and suggests that postmodern and electronic culture share some similarities with the premodern and oral culture. While it is helpful to use oral culture as a means to reflect on electronic culture, it is important not to see electronic culture and visualization as simply a return to more primal forms of life. There are real differences in these practices. Try to imagine, for example, the sensuous difference in working with a computer and screen and operating in an oral culture that does not have a written language. Snyder, of course, knows this, but I say it so that it is clear that electronic culture is not simply some reprise of orality.

Still, learning from oral culture can help one to think about our own time in a different way. I am struck again by Anyanwu's comment about traditional Africa, in which sound is the model of reality and the criterion of truth. Only in this connection it seems that visualization also provides this function for increasing numbers of people born since World War II in the United States. Moreover, when one realizes how much sound as beat and visualization are combined in electronic culture, one begins to gain some sense of the power of these dynamics and the increasing role they play in knowing and in forming what are regarded as reliable guides for people in everyday life.

The coming of visualization does not mean that sound as beat is disappearing, but that the visual as visualization is taking on a prominence it has not had in these terms. It is not so much the loss of sound as beat, but rather the emerging importance of visualization in relation to beat that results in the increasing importance of the screen. Beat itself has changed with this shift.

Visualization As Percussive

Testimony to the continuing importance of sound is the influence it has on visualization. I think particularly of how percussive it has become. The pulsing beat of light, images, and video techniques is now basic to an enormous range of movies, concerts, and screen presentations.

One of the most interesting of these is Michael Jackson's introduction to his Greatest Hits video. The introduction is not really Jackson's singing. In fact, the music is *Carmina Burana,* composed by Carl Orff in 1935–1936. Orff based his composition on poems from the thirteenth century found at the abbey of Nenediktbeuren in 1803. These poems dealt a frontal attack on the Church, medieval manners and morals, and money, while casting lilting, driving, rhythmic praise on the sensuality of food, wine, and erotic love.

Published as a manuscript in 1847 by Johann Andreas Schmeller with the title "Carmina Burana" ("Songs of Beuren"), Orff took selections from these poems and put them to music, a feat that Hanspeter Krellmann explains in *The New Grove Dictionary:* "Orff's main concern is not with the exposition of human nature in tragedy, nor with whimsical fancy, nor with the statement of supernatural truths, nor with joyous exultation. His intention seems to be to create a spectacle."[9]

Certainly, this seems to be the purpose for Michael Jackson's use of it. The video begins with Orff's music percussively depicting Jackson in a major concert with short sound bite images of him in quickly changing contexts. He is at one moment flying in on an airplane, in another meeting fans, and then walking with police as he apparently enters the stadium. The scenery picks up speed as he performs in concert with an audience that is enrapt. We see audience members moving, dancing, crying, and showing anguished and yearning expressions filled with adoration of Jackson. In this display, pounding rhythmic light and the use of cut images are sequenced so as to punctuate glimpses of his show and of the audience, and these in turn increase in rapidity, becoming more vibrant and cadenced with the driving pulse of Orff's composition. Onstage the electronic lights throb and explode to the beat of the music. Then to accentuate the light, fireworks go off, again at the climax of *Carmina Burana*'s turns, which are electronically coordinated with Jackson's moves and the audience's engrossed, spectacular engagement. The piece moves to its end with Jackson transposed into a cruciform explosion of light.

It is difficult to watch a video like Jackson's and not see how much sound as beat influences visualization. While it seems clear that the ratio of the visual to sound has shifted, it would be a mistake of the first order to think that the place of beat is no longer central to electronic culture and its popular expression. I realize, of course, that not all uses of the screen make beat this central, but the same tactic is employed in the theme music to TV shows like "NYPD Blue," and as we see in Jackson's video it is the staple of concerts and music video.

Image, Beat, and Visualization

It is obvious in the Michael Jackson video that one is not dealing with visualization alone. The central involvement of image and sound as beat cannot be missed. It is important, then, not to treat image, beat, and visualization as abstractions either in themselves or in separation from one another if they are to be understood in terms of the place they now have in this culture and the power they represent in the practices basic to contemporary forms of life. Indeed, it is in their combination that one gets the clearest picture/rhythm/screening of their power.

In this connection, it is a mistake to understand these events as the culture industries and mass media imposing themselves unilaterally on passive (consumerist) audiences, especially in concerts. Such views not only fail to see the way that people use such events but also do not grasp a powerful intrinsic function at work here. It is not only what the culture industries and performers produce; it is what is enacted by the crowds. It is what they bring to the event. It is what emerges in these settings where images, sound as beat, and visualization as key components in the performance of these entertainers become occasions in which highly ritualized activity occurs, activity that is emergent in this process and not reducible to any of its components alone.

The bad rap against many of these spectacles is that they represent a distorted view of the real world. As we see above with Baudrillard, such events create a world that is more real than real, a world of hyperreality, the presentation of a copy without an original, meaning that there is no reference in the actual world to what is happening before an audience.

One can certainly make this case with the Michael Jackson video. The music, for example, is not his and is not something he does in concert. A moment's reflection reminds us that Orff's *Carmina Burana* sounds nothing like Jackson's "Billie Jean." Moreover, the images of Jackson, his band, and the crowd edited and percussively used to accentuate the beat of Orff's composition are not seen by concert attenders, although buyers of the video do, of course, view them. At the end of the piece Jackson himself explodes into a cruciform of light, suggesting a metaphor that leaves us puzzled about his reality. Is this some not so subtle attempt to make him the electronic savior, or does the fact that the cross of light floats at an angle indicate that we are to put together the lyric contents of the *Songs of Buren* and to see Jackson as some more exquisite exemplifier of the misdeeds of those thirteenth-century monks? Is it simply an artful way to place this luminous cross in a video and really meant "only" to divinize Jackson, or is it something else? Are we giving it too much thought, making too much of it? The point is that Baudrillard, no matter what is intended, would have a field day with the Jackson video.

Still, I do not think this is an adequate treatment of what goes on in concerts and in a host of electronic practices. While I have no patience with the theological pretensions of Michael Jackson, if that's what they are, Baudrillard's approach to videos as distortive representations is not adequate. In Jackson's video, however, it would be hard to deny that no little blurred focus goes on, if not outright fabrications of a never, never world.

At the same time, it is crucial to remember that image, sound as beat, and visualization are not only presentations by a performer or performers, they are also occasions for the enactment of experience by participants and by large crowds who gather. In this context, image, beat, and visualization do not equal experience; they do not reduce understanding to the spectacle; they do not equal the meaning of the event. These await the enactment of the gathering.

For this reason I turn toward practices related most directly to image, beat, and visualization because of the special role they have assumed and the significant dynamics that now take place around them. I think here particularly of the practices most evident in concerts, but not only there, and of the crucial role that image, beat, and visualization play in the dynamics of bonding, commitment, identity formation, and that elusive matter we call meaning. These are questions of the first order if we are to examine the indigenous practices of an electronic culture. These questions will engage us next.

CHAPTER FIVE

Indigenous Practices in an Electronic Culture: Spectacle and Performance

Peggy and I sailed into Istanbul late one afternoon. (We don't go to Istanbul a lot.) We wanted to see some traditional forms of Turkish culture. We were told that the only place giving performances so late in the day was the evening show at the Galata Tower, a supper club not far from the seaport where we arrived. So that evening we and our friends, Tom and Fran Manson, went. It was a wonderful presentation, and while the traditional dances and music had a kind of professional polish to them, we nevertheless enjoyed our time there.

I had heard that the finale of the show would feature the headliner and star of the evening, a man we understood to be a kind of Turkish appropriation of the combined styles of Tony Bennett, Dean Martin, and Frank Sinatra. After the program had been going for about an hour and a half, I began to think about the fact that this performer would have to come out near the end of the evening and entertain an international audience. Since I do a good deal of public speaking, I reflected on how difficult it must be to get up at the end of a two-hour show and provide a climax to a very nice time. So far we had been privileged to see and hear local songs and dances. His job, we had been told, was to provide a more contemporary Las Vegas-style performance.

I began to worry for him. What would I do facing a group of people from a diversity of nations? How could I connect with them? Even if I had good humor (often not the case), it doesn't translate across

54

culture. I must confess it ruined the last fifteen minutes of the show before his act because I became so concerned for him!

When we came in earlier that evening, the maître d' had asked which country we were from, and when we told him, he placed an American flag at our table. I noticed from the flags on the tables that there were people from Austria, Israel, and Italy around us. I deemed the flags a nice touch, but did not give it much thought.

When the headliner came out, he made a very dramatic entrance, complete with an augmented and percussive use of lighting, which is commonplace at such events. His act was obviously significant. He immediately launched into a fast-paced, rhythmic song with a strong upbeat, which picked up the mood of the entire room. The lighting pulsed with the music and a strong bass beat got everything moving. It was a good start.

From this he went into a ballad about romantic love, a slow and easy 4/4. He was a very handsome man, and he established immediate rapport with the women in the room. Men like me, of course, identified with his aura of good looks, as though what he possessed made up for what we lacked. He was doing well.

From the ballad he moved to another fast-paced soft rock tune, and he had us again. Still, I thought to myself, "This is good but he can't keep doing this. If he keeps going from ballad to upbeat songs and back again, it won't work."

As my worry and apprehension for him mounted, he moved to the next song. As he did so, he came down from the stage into the audience and began the lyrics to "Volaré." With that, the Italians at the next table jumped to their feet and began to sing the chorus with him. He walked toward them and put the microphone in front of one man. Whatever that man lacked in vocal quality, he more than made up for in an excess of enthusiasm. The Italians waved their arms, danced to the tune, and waxed ecstatic over this artistic representation of their culture, their country, and their music.

After three verses and choruses to "Volaré" that had all the character of a pep rally, he shifted to "Edelweiss." It became the Austrians' turn. He sang and they joined in, as he shared the mike once again. With boisterous Austrian loyalty they rang the rafters with "Bloom and grow for ever. Edelweiss, Edelweiss, Bless my homeland forever."[1]

The music then transitioned to "La Chaim," and, as soon as the tune was recognized, the Israelis went wild. They did some constrained—by table space—version of a traditional dance and shouted the strength of choosing life into the microphone, which had been given over to their fervent rendition of soul music.

At this point I have to report that the singer did not really understand the culture of the United States. He chose a song that he believed would ignite our American table as he had the others. But he chose the wrong song, clearly not soul music. He started the lyrics to "New York! New York!" Well, any half-sentient midwesterner understands the cultural fluff of both seacoasts in the United States. The substance of our country is in its heartland, not in the faddish flim-flam of the neomania coming from the "Big Apple" and San Francisco. The music should be "Kansas City, Here I Come."

To make matters worse, he stuck the microphone in front of me. Well, I have made a moral and religious point of not memorizing a song of such obvious inconsequence. Of course, I couldn't go into the argument necessary to communicate the dire nature of his error in this context. So I simply mouthed the fact that I did not know the words, since I dared not speak out loud with the microphone in my face. From him I got a look of utter incredulity that stopped him momentarily from continuing with the lyric. He recovered and moved to Peggy, who has pipes.

Peggy ripped two lines from the song. He knew what he had, so he took her up on stage and they sang the finale together, belting out Neeewwwwww Yooorrrrrk! Nuuuuoooooowww Yooooooorrrrrrrk! With that they brought the house down and ended the evening.

I think about that evening often. It was a good learning moment, because it expressed very basic practices of an electronic culture as seen in an entertainment setting.

First, it clearly showed the power of popular culture in an international context. It was not lost on us that the United States has had great influence on "soul music" even in Istanbul. But the influence of the popular culture of the United States has become a global phenomenon.

Second, it is an expression of what is often called "spectacle." While it was certainly not on the scale of a concert by Michael Jackson, Tina Turner, Garth Brooks, Reba McEntire, The Grateful Dead, or Nirvana, it certainly was a spectacle. Even more, it was not a spectacle aimed at the younger generations, except for the older Boomers who were there. While the music often had a pronounced upbeat to it, it was clearly aimed at the more affluent upper-middle-class travelers who gathered there every night, who are typically older.

Spectacles are not new to the world. They've been around a long time. And they, indeed, have a checkered history. One thinks of the Roman world and the arena at the beginning of the common era, where sometimes Christians and others were thrown to the lions. Or one moves to the twentieth century and Nuremberg where Hitler and his Nazis put on display the power of the Third Reich. Yet, such violations do not necessarily characterize spectacles. Today, tractor pulls, sports events like the Olympics, special occasions at state fairs, political conventions, July Fourth celebrations, college and professional football and basketball games and other events fall into the category of spectacles.

Early in this century Emile Durkheim, the great French sociologist, observed that when you get people in close physical proximity to one another, focus their attention on a common object, and engage them in exercises that arouse emotion, bonding occurs.[2] Such dynamics play powerful roles in the bonding of people across a range of cultures and history. Such is the power of spectacle, and more, as we shall see presently.

There was no little bonding and sense of our collaborative spirit in that supper club that evening, and there were a góod many informal expressions of it, though no one so far as I know gave it more substance than it deserved. But I do remember the strong sense of camaraderie and togetherness I experienced at the end of a delightful evening.

The Bad Rap on Spectacle

Spectacle is a basic and indigenous practice in electronic culture whenever we find a full-blown use of image, sound as beat, and visualization. Indeed, it is the augmented power of these electronic factors that enhances a spectacle's capacity and makes it even more captivating.

Serious questions have been raised about spectacle. Spectacle is said to deflect the attention of people away from the real issues of society. Our evening at the Galata Tower hardly led us to address the issues of whether those serving us were adequately compensated for their efforts. Nothing on that occasion raised questions among the international, affluent, upper-middle-class audience members who were able to use Greece, Turkey, Israel, Italy, or Austria as a vacation playground. Our bonding and camaraderie were based in no substantive engagement with one another that could lead to anything more than feeling good during an evening out in "exotic" Istanbul.

These kinds of questions are exactly the kind that critics of spectacle raise about practices that increasingly characterize an electronic culture.

Certainly no one raises these questions more sharply than Marxists, and perhaps the best exponent of this critique is Guy Debord in his important book *The Society of the Spectacle*. He tells us in one of its prefaces that the book is "written with the deliberate intention of doing harm to spectacular society."[3] For him spectacle is a social relationship mediated by images. It is a worldview that is now a part of "concrete lived life" (my language). It is the outcome and goal of economic forces, but it is not "a decorative element" but rather "the very heart of society's real unreality."[4] At this point his position is close to that of Baudrillard's. For Debord the spectacle is a result of real activity, but it creates appearances that make falsehood seem more real than actual life.

For example, in the warm confines of the Galata Tower we engaged in real activity: music, dancing, singing our national songs, and finding an international bonding and good community. My memories of Istanbul are crowded with that evening. My images of Istanbul are full of that night. But how much is the spectacle of that evening actually related to what goes on in Turkey? Was our evening "real" or was it a diversion, actually an emotive and "inspirational" evening that made it virtually impossible to get some more accurate idea of what goes on there? Even more important in terms of our responsibilities for our own lives, were we lulled into a "feel good internationalism" that simply was unrelated to global issues of justice? For example, we never saw any poverty in Istanbul, though it is clearly there. Spectacles can blind us to such questions.

I am not trying to condemn celebrative life. Clearly one does not have to sit around and commiserate about the evils of the world all the time, and I do not feel guilty about a fun evening in Istanbul. No one can be more grim than some Marxists. If conservative Republicans have one corner of the market on anal-retentive theory and behavior, then certainly some Marxists have another. But Marxists help us see that spectacle can divert us from a world that may not have to be addressed at every waking moment of our lives, but also must not be ignored or papered over.

One of the problems with some Marxists is that they give productive practices so central a place that they do not adequately address cultural practices. In chapter 1 I indicate how much we are shaped physically, mentally, emotionally, and sensually by the basic practices that constitute our lives. We have seen how our knowing and what we regard as cogent or telling or authentic or true are conditioned by practices that "wire us" (encode us) and attune us to a world that is profoundly constructed historically and culturally.

Thus we examine the indigenous practices of a culture or a cultural formation to gain some acquaintance with it. Karl Marx made the point of how important our *productive* practices are in forming our lives. He saw clearly how dull, monotonous, routine, repetitive, laborious work—done under the coercive, exploitative structure of life and production in the economic order of his time—led to the alienation of people from themselves, from their related workers, from work, from their products, indeed from life itself. His description of the poverty of the working classes of London in the middle of the nineteenth century remains to this day a classic testimony to the brutality of that era and to the impact of productive relations and their practices on the vast majority of human beings.[5]

I sympathize with this drudgery because, in the text that follows, I do not want to forget the powerful influence that one's work or unemployment or poverty and the practices attendant to it play in the shaping of one's life. In fact, I want to learn the practices of an electronic culture, in part, so that these crucial issues can be more effectively addressed.

Marx's focus was almost exclusively on productive relations and practices. He worked with a sharp distinction between the economic base (the productive relations and practices) and the superstructure (the realm of the state, law, family, religion, ideology, et al.).

For example, if a society has as a basic tool a digging stick, then its farming, really its gardening, would be radically affected by that tooling.[6]

In such a society the size of a farm would be small, and the practices of farming would be profoundly conditioned by that kind of small-scale tooling. It would affect property relationships. There would be no large farms, for example. Kinship would be ordered to deal with the necessities of this form of life. The kind of religious expression would be oriented to this life. Law would be sculpted to address the issues arising from this set of relationships. In Marx's terms, the base is constituted by the tooling, the relationships developed around it, the practices made necessary by it, and so on. The superstructure would be the state, the law, religion, ideology, and so forth, which are outgrowths of these material means of production.

With only a minute's reflection, one can see how radically this all changes if one introduces a tractor with a gasoline or diesel engine that can pull plows that cultivate twelve or more rows at a time. An economic base of this kind has enormous impact on the superstructure. Take this one more step to a society with electronic technology and, again, one can see how powerfully this tooling and the material means of production change life and shape it.

Hence Marx sees the superstructure as basically mirroring or reflecting the material means of production or the economic base. It is a brilliant formulation, and one that explains much about a society. Nevertheless, he did not give adequate attention to other practices, such as cultural ones of a non-economic kind, and their formative role, except as reflections of the more basic economic realities.[7]

This kind of materialist thinking is clearly reflected in Debord's understanding. While he sees spectacle as real activity, as we see above, it is clear that culture is a mirroring of more basic economic realities. For example, he defines culture as "the general sphere of knowledge, and of representations of lived experience, within a historical society divided into classes." This means that "culture is the power to generalize, existing *apart,* as an intellectual division of labor and as the intellectual labor of division."[8]

Culture is reduced by Debord to intellectual activity, a notion that erases a host of other practices across an enormous range of concrete lived life. Raymond Williams, however, demonstrates that cultural activity must be seen and understood in terms of the ways it is produced and reproduced. When examining spectacle it is not enough to analyze the influences of economic factors, but it must be understood in terms of its own concrete practices and how these shape our lives in their own terms.[9]

Spectacle gets a one-sided treatment in Marxist thought when it is seen as an aspect of the superstructure, and hence merely as a reflection of economic factors. It therefore is not seen in terms of the more positive role it can play. In popular culture, spectacle presently is a central practice. It needs close examination in its concrete practices.

Spectacles are capable of enormous harm. I remember a lecture once by Professor Edwin Prince Booth at the Boston University School of Theology. He told us of being a graduate student in Germany during the 1930s and going to hear Hitler speak at Nuremberg, a spectacle if there ever was one. Booth stated that in the United States in those years imitations of Hitler were done in which his speech and mannerisms were derisively stereotyped and demeaned. Booth, however, argued that such satirical treatments never engaged the power of Hitler's oratory, which Booth described as "torrential eloquence." Booth said that while he sharply disagreed with everything Hitler said, he still chilled with the emotional captivation of the event. Such is the demonic capacity of spectacle.

At the same time, to focus only on the evil capacities of spectacles is to miss the contributions they can make. I think here, for example, of the use of spectacle as an alternative or resistant or subversive event. In terms of the church such use of spectacle seems to be especially important.

Spectacle As Performance

As I sat in the Galata Tower supper club, I watched carefully the performance of the star of the evening. By the time he came on, the audience had been readied for his entrance. Later as I thought about the evening, I realized the star had followed three basic steps in ensuring his success. First, although the show had gone on for nearly two hours, we were eagerly awaiting his appearance. I couldn't help thinking about how often worship in the church begins "cold" with very little, if any, preparation. At the time, I remembered going to many concerts where the star had another performer "warm-up" the crowd first. It is a basic practice in performance.

Second, I noticed how he used pacing. By beginning with a fast-moving song with a solid beat and using light percussively to augment the moment, he lent credence to the expectation that we were not going to be disappointed in his time with us. But he knew we would not stay with a continuous diet of fast-paced songs even by a performer as professional as he clearly was. When he moved to a ballad as his second piece, he changed pace. With that the rhythm of the performance shifted. The light did not pulse but rather stopped, except to focus on him and to darken the rest of the room and the stage. There was no screen in the room of any kind, but the visualization was present in the use of lights to focus on the singer at one moment and members of the band at others. This focus moved and kept the attention of the audience shifting with the pace of the song and the performance.

Third, his move to include the participation of the audience was one of the best things he did. His use of songs representing the different countries in the room was certainly a deft move, but when he moved down into the audience and began to share that microphone, he had us! The fact that some of us sing so poorly did not hurt the moment but enhanced it, offering humor that seemed to solidify us all the more. When he took Peggy up on the stage, it seemed to me like the entire crowd wanted to identify with her and she became the representative "star" in us all.

We were in the presence of an accomplished performer, one who knew exactly what he had to do to claim and sustain the involvement of an international audience. His performance included the use of fast-paced images and beat, and his use of lights gave a moving visualization and pulse to the event. Yet, he clearly understood the importance of pacing, the rhythm of the performance, and the participation of the audience. His performance had the character of a spectacle, albeit on a smaller scale. It is a sharp reminder that performance is a basic aspect of spectacle, but also a basic practice of electronic culture in its own right.

CHAPTER SIX

Indigenous Practices in an Electronic Culture: Soul Music and Dance

If spectacle and performance are basic indigenous practices in an electronic culture, it should be quite clear that music, more precisely soul music, will be such a practice also.

Sound and Light

Walter Ong claims that sound conveys meaning more powerfully and accurately than does sight.[1] Stated in these terms, Ong's comment comes off as ahistorical and without context. At the same time, I trust Ong's insight enough to believe that he does point to something that has been true of sound in the West. Will this always be so? What is the relation of sound and sight in music as a practice in contemporary electronic culture, and what forms it is now taking?

Music is a central practice in electronic culture, but to equate it with sound alone is to overlook image and visualization, which are so often used in musical performance. Image and light are now percussive in their use. In a sense, image and light imitate sound.

Consider African drumming. African drumming is "polyrhythmic." It has rich complexity and "the dynamic clash and interplay of cross rhythms," says John Chernoff.[2] Mickey Hart, the percussionist for the Grateful Dead notes that African drumming will often use "three or four different rhythms occurring at any one time."[3] Tricia Rose in her

63

fine book on rap music points to similar characteristics of African drumming:

> Rhythm and polyrhythmic layering is [*sic*] to African and African-derived musics what harmony and the harmonic triad is [*sic*] to Western classical music. Dense configurations of independent, but closely related, rhythms, harmonic and nonharmonic percussive sounds, especially drum sounds, are critical priorities in many African and Afrodiasporic musical practices.[4]

These discussions of African music are important because there has been a significant "blackening" of popular music in the U.S. through the influence of African American rhythmic and percussive forms. This influence can now be seen not only in sound but in visualization. For example, music in electronic spectacles now uses not only polyrhythmic beat, but light in similar multirhythmic and layering ways. Pulsing illumination employed in this layering fashion sweeps an audience. This constitutes not only a shift in the use of light, but a change in the character of music and its more basic association to sound. Of course, visuality has always had an important relation to music. I have certainly thrilled to watch a symphony moving together in that driving conclusion wrestling toward resolution. But here I see new forms of the use of image and visualization integrated with sound in music through percussion.

A number of writers, including Ong, note that sound "enters" us in a way that the visual cannot.[5] I believe this has now shifted so that the percussive character of light now accompanying sound takes on a role and importance it has not had before. This qualifies Ong's insight. Light has come to take on something like the character of sound. In this connection, compare the place volume and light now have within much popular music, especially in concert. In electronic spectacles beat "enters" one's body. You can actually feel the vibration against your skin, muscle, and bone. Changes, however, in visualization now provide a parallel result with the visual. You cannot simply close your eyes and block out the stimulation. The detonations of light penetrate eyelids and percussively illuminate the arena around you. Our capacity to shut out the visual, should one want to, has become more limited.

This light augments music and gives it a multisensory character of a kind it has not had prior to electronic culture. A practitioner as sophisticated as Mickey Hart says that he is "synesthetic, which means I see sounds and hear images."[6]

Soul Music

This encoding is synthesized as soul music in terms of image, beat, and visualization. Soul music is not merely tunes and lyrics that one prefers. It has at least three levels. One level is very much connected to the kind of encoding that has occurred among people of a particular soul music. It is easy to forget how much our subjectivity is imputed from our cultural and historical socialization. We are formed by them. When a music is basic to this encoding, it becomes soul music. This means it is not merely pleasant, but "touches" and fulfills the sensory and feeling character of the encoding.

These are not superficial sensory and feeling qualities. We have misled ourselves in the West and in the United States by believing we have universal feelings and senses and ways of knowing, and that these are merely unfolded in history somehow. I am suggesting something quite different. We have no set human nature in these terms. Rather, these characteristics are hammered out in history, and the wonderful plasticity of human beings is shaped in the flow of these events. What seems increasingly clear is that these terribly intimate characteristics are quite particular and deeply ingrained—read as enculturated—in us and that we share these intersubjectively with others who are part of our cultural and historical experience.

This brings us to another level or dimension of music with important consequences for soul. The music of the world can be seen as traditions.[7] Soul music reflects a tradition. I do not mean here that there is some range of essence that a tradition fulfills. Rather, across a time and in a social location, conventions in music are developed that express a tradition and in turn encode the people of that tradition.

Hence a soul music is constituted of the tunes, the lyrics, and the rhythms of a people. But these have also participated in the very creation of the people so represented. These have been conventionalized—I don't mean made staid and stale, though this happens, but creatively constructed—so that they come to reflect the lives of the people, on the one hand, and become the occasion for enacting these lives, on the other.

Sometimes a new music will burst on the scene and suddenly take on great significance. It seems to "name" the lives of the people committed to it. No music, of course, is utterly new. Rather, "new" music seems to incorporate a number of existing elements in some new synthesis, some new "statement" of expression and identity that "says" it, that enacts people's lives. Rap music, for example, seems to have done this for many urban young people when it came on the public scene in the late 1970s. In the case of rap, it emerged on the streets of major urban centers.[8]

Soul music is as deep as muscle and bone, as intimate as feeling, and as close cognitively as the way we know the world around us. The word *soul,* then, is a good one because music of this kind is profoundly bound up with one's very being.

Moreover, the nature of music is shifting right before our eyes and ears. The new relationship between music and beat and light, which has come into being since World War II, represents a new emergent not previously available. New traditions have been forming. Music will never be the same. In this connection I have not mentioned the new instruments developed in an electronic culture. These both express these new traditions and enact them.

Music and Narrative

It should not be surprising then that the music of popular culture has taken a relatively new role in everyday life.

In her study of music in the English town of Milton Keynes, Ruth Finnegan maintains, quite effectively, that what people do with their free time in both leisure pursuits and volunteer activities is more important in shaping their "pathways" than what they do for a living.[9] This declaration is a good corrective to a Marxist position that focuses too exclusively on productive relations and sees cultural practices as too simply reflective of more basic economic relations and activity.

Finnegan also discovered that the people of Milton Keynes found their most compelling narratives in musical activities. In a word, this means that great numbers of people find the story for their lives in the soul music that speaks to and of them. I remember a grandmother who struggled most of her life. She bore nine children and worked outside the home much of her life. Her "career" started out cooking in a caboose on the railroad for men working on the line. Her husband was an expert in assessing how much timber stood on an acreage, a skill that put him in a valuable place with the yellow pine industry in Mississippi in the 1930s and 1940s. When he was sober, they did well,

66

but he was regularly drunk. He was also a womanizer. I remember times when she would be facing one more extremely difficult situation, but she always seemed like a rock. In those hard times she would without fail sing to herself any time she had a semiprivate moment. One of her favorite songs was "Jesus, Savior, Pilot Me." She could be sowing, washing dishes, sweeping, working outside, in reverie, or crushed with sadness, but she would sing that song, half to herself, half out loud. That song, the Jesus story told in the hymn, held her together. It was decidedly her soul music and the story that named her life and kept her struggling in a world that would not come out right.

But listen to a new rendition. My students and I were working in class one day on rap music and its relationship to the African American community. We were especially interested in its role in the lives of Black youth. Ed Jones, a tall, handsome man who had come into ministry after a career as a firefighter, broke in.

"Tex, can I give a testimony here?"

When we all gave an affirmative response, he stood up at his desk like a man at a revival about to tell of meeting Jesus and being saved. He stated, "In 1979 I had never heard of rap music in my entire life. I was a kid in Houston, Texas, when for the first time I heard The Sugarhill Gang do 'Rapper's Delight.' I knew instantly that it had always been my music, though I had never heard it before, and it would always be my music. Nothing has ever so touched me or so fully said who I am."

I think often of my grandmother and Ed. In her case her "theology," really her story, came from the hymnody. In this respect she was typical of many people of her generation. The hymnody provided their "theology" and shaped their spirituality. Grandma prayed the hymn. For Ed rap music plays this role. I don't mean to suggest that the Jesus story is not important to him or that gospel and other forms of music are not. They clearly are. But the Jesus story takes on a soul-full embodiment in Ed through the music that has since scored him with its sound, beat, and visualization. Rap is his soul music and names his life. As a result, he has for several years been working on the use of rap and other contemporary music for worship because he believes it is an essential music to people he wants to reach.

If Finnegan is correct, and I think she is, Ed shares a significant relationship with many other people in American society, especially those born after World War II. The case can be made, appropriately, that people have had soul music throughout the history of the U.S., but I think the form of soul music for most people under the age of fifty has changed. It will sound and *look* different now than it did before. It has taken on rhythmic and illuminative qualities it has not had, and it is expressed through popular forms.

Aesthetics and Ethics

Finnegan found that people in her study gave expression to their basic ethical stances in and through aesthetic judgments. While some will bemoan such emergent patterns, and we do not have to be uncritical of them, I am interested in the new context that a soul music may bring to the work of ethics.[10]

Perhaps two illustrations will help. The first is a nonmusical one. I will never forget the time when Will Campbell, that wonderful self-proclaimed "Baptist of the South," was in a radio debate on the death penalty. His opponent had the first presentation and laid out as much of his position as he could in the few minutes he had, quoting statistics and making as many arguments as possible. The moderator then turned to Will and asked him for his opening statement. Will simply said: "The death penalty is tacky," and stopped. The moderator asked if that was all he had to say, and Will said it was. The moderator tried again and said, "Well, Will, we know that the word 'tacky' means inappropiate, unseemly, and ugly." "That's right," said Will, "and that's my argument." Needless to say it was a showstopper. It was also a direct appeal to aesthetics.

If you know Will Campbell, you can understand that a move like this could be a ploy, but you also know that he is *dead* serious about the tackiness of the death penalty. For him capital punishment is intrinsically wrong and intrinsically ugly. Should he use such a claim as a ploy, an extrinsic move that would use the aesthetic judgment as a means for winning a debate, it is only because he believes this legal sentence is indiscriminately nasty, hideous, and repulsive in itself.

But in the second illustration Will makes the case in the more positive direction as well. To see and hear Will sit in a chair and sing country music songs in order to make commentary on contemporary events is to witness a sensitive and compassionate beauty, as compelling an ethical "argument" as I have ever heard. With people for whom country is their soul music, it has a "cogency" commensurate with any literate tour de force and touches those—now apparently a growing majority—whom more theoretical and conceptual ethical claims leave cold and unmoved.

It should also be obvious that these developments in soul music have enormous capacities for misuse. A music that can be embodied through image, beat, and visualization that can touch more of a person's constructed life, a music that offers the compelling narrative of a tradition and a music that makes claims for aesthetic beauty as an intrinsic display of the right and the good, of justice and peace, are all subject to the most violative kinds of distortion and demonic captivity. These dangers are intensified in a consumer society. Complacency about such hazards is no answer. But such ambiguity seems to come with any cultural formation. It is not something we can finally escape, but rather something that we must resist, counter, and subvert.

I suggest that the use of image, beat, and visualization has encoded younger generations in new ways, and that music traditions reflect and enact soul. These are new formations with new practices. Nothing, however, completes this embodiment more than dance and its important role in spectacle and electronic culture.

Dance

Peggy and I arrived an hour-and-a-half before the performance. When we parked twenty rows back in a huge parking lot I realized we had underestimated how early we needed to be there. The Sandstone Amphitheater is a large open-air arena with stadium-like seats near the stage that number several thousand. We bought our tickets six weeks before, but these seats were already sold out. So we took our place on the ground on the grassy hillside section behind the more "intimate" stadium-like area. Even then we are forty yards back on the grass.

We had our blanket down and our lawn chairs in place. A young woman came in, put her blanket on the ground, and said to no one in particular: "Folks, I want you to know that when the show starts, I'll be standing the whole time. I just don't want anybody to misunderstand."

"Then, dear, you had better look a lot like Tina Turner," I said, suggesting more than I knew about how out of touch I was with what was about to happen.

The young woman immediately got up and moved! I often wonder what kind of grinch she thought I was. Later on I will agree with whatever her conclusion happens to be.

Cyndi Lauper did the warm-up performance. She knows how to do it. Not only did the pacing and rhythm disclose her knowledge of how to work an audience, but she also used her ability to gain the participation of the people there in order to build the excitement. At one point she was not satisfied with the response she was getting, so she took the mike and ran down into the audience singing to and with people within a hundred-foot area. It ignited the crowd.

This was the Tina Turner tour of 1997 and we gathered to see, hear, and watch this ecstatic fifty-eight-year-old wonder sing, dance, explode, and sparkle and spangle before our eyes for two whole hours. Three twenty-something women backed her up on stage as singers and dancers, but none of them outmoved her, outdanced her, outlasted her. Meanwhile two large video screens on each side and at the top of the stage fired images at us. At one moment, we saw the performance from different visual standpoints on the stage. At other times, the video took us back in Turner's past and flashed footage of her singing the same songs earlier in her career.

And, of course, as soon as the Turner show began, the crowd was on their feet and dancing throughout the evening. I did too. I continually fought my encoded tendencies to emphasize the downbeat, which did not work. I felt like the church, a downbeat institution in an upbeat world. In front of me was a teenager, about seventeen, I guess. She was fluent in image, beat, and visualization, and she danced as though her central nervous system was directly wired to Tina Turner and the entire spectacle around her. "It is time for apprenticeship!" I said to myself. I then began that sincerest form of flattery, imitation. With that I danced for two hours, interrupted only by an occasional need to sit and rest, a generational concession, I concluded, in spite of the uncompromising example of Tina Turner.

It is clear in these moments that dance is an indigenous practice in electronic culture. Such a claim need not deny the importance dance has in other times and places. In the pulsing sound and light of Turner's concert, in the complex visuals taking one's focus from here to there and somewhere else again, in the pace and rhythm of the performance itself taking us from "On Silent Wings" to "Proud Mary," in the incessant movement onstage and in the audience, a convergence begins that can only be completed in dance, and communal dance at that. Such fullness of ear and eye, of feeling and sense, and yes, even of taste, smell, and touch, can only finally be expressed in the full kinesthetic action of the body, in dance. Even I, as electronically challenged as I am, can at least "see" that this is so.

It is clear, too, that a kind of transcendence is at work here. One is taken out of the ordinary, routine world in these moments. It is another time and place. It has a spiritual and meditative quality about it. I suppose I could get righteous and declare it an idolatrous excursion in entertainment, sound, screen, dance, and tribal excesses. But it does not seem so much idolatrous as the telling of a host of stories, stories of loss and hope, of yearning and fulfillment, of longing and of resolution. Turner's rendition of "On Silent Wings" hammers out in a continual beat but in a ballad form the message that relationships can be devastatingly cruel, that something intimately good can die, and that love can slip away on silent wings. Many people hear their story in her story. When she counters that with a song, "Something Beautiful Remains," there is a gathering of the pieces to put life back together and to go on. Desperate loss and embers of hope are juxtaposed in a display of multisensory liturgy and dance, which gives kinesthetic expression to a total-body engagement.

Dance and the Church

Dance as an indigenous practice in electronic culture is a major challenge to most churches today. While dance has played an important role in Scripture and in church history, at least in some traditions, it is virtually not a practice in most churches except when done occasionally by one or more "liturgical dancers." I believe it needs to be developed much more, not only as done by a few performers, but as congregational dance.

In this connection I am struck by the work of Marcia McFee, a theologically trained dancer. I am continually amazed at what she can do with staid, rock-still congregations to get them moving and yes, even dancing, in worship. It is not only that she is a fine dancer, having danced for six years with Dave Brubeck and his quartet, but that she understands why she is engaged in leading people in worship. I remember seeing a local pastor on Monday after she had been at his church the previous Sunday morning. When I asked how things had gone in worship with Marcia, he answered that he thought she must have hurt his people. When I asked in a worried way what had happened, he laughed and said, "They moved!"

If you ask Marcia for some basic instruction in using dance in worship, she offers the following, which I will mainly list as a first step in getting people involved.

1. First, begin with movement, not necessarily dance. She says that sometimes this means simply clapping hands or, in the case of those challenged in overt behavior, that they simply pat their toes inside their shoes to the beat.

2. Don't create movement extraneous to the people's experience. She tries to "read" a congregation and use moves and steps that are within their basic practices, if not in worship, then in their everyday lives.

3. Prepare people verbally for the symbolism involved in an action. This will not only legitimate the effort, but give it the appropriate purpose that worship requires.

4. Marcia observes that there are four basic rhythmic actions that work well: "stomping," snapping fingers, slapping the thigh or knee, and clapping. These will typically get any congregation "moving."

5. She calls special attention to the semiotics of dance. Semiotics is the study of signs, and in this context she is talking about the meaning conveyed through signs in dance. It is important, obviously, that people have some understanding of these signs, although Marcia's moves seem to communicate "naturally" through dance. The danger for interpreters of movement is to associate only one sign to a theological concept, thereby limiting the ways we experience the Divine. To convey the expansiveness of God, she suggests not only wide-open motions, but a huddled position that can communicate a closeness, a womblike feeling, the immanence of the Divine. By falling into and then pushing away from a wall, one can indicate resistance to the forces of evil and the subsequent release in freedom or joy.

Often one sees liturgical dancers express emotion like pain

or despair or grief with overly large movements of the hands and arms over the head and bowed down in heavy-laden postures. Marcia suggests instead that these may be best captured in small, subtle movements. She says, for example, that a small, quick jerk of the torso in or backward conveys pain powerfully.

I am especially struck by what she says about the semiotics of contemporary dance in the expression of jubilant feeling. To embody joy and delight in God, she suggests "crazy" shapes to signify the sense that nothing is adequate to it. She also notes that in analyzing the motions of our everyday lives, the communication of joy is usually typified in downward movements: a "belly laugh," stamping the feet, slapping the knee, and reaching the hand up and bringing it down in a sudden *yes* action.

6. In contemporary dance, Marcia observes, the direction is to get back to the earth, not to leave it. As an illustration, Peggy and I were fortunate to attend a ballet at the Bolshoi in Moscow in November, 1995. Before we left the U.S. I had had a meeting with Marcia about dance and she made the comment about contemporary dance getting back to the earth, so it was very much on my mind.

At the Bolshoi that evening we witnessed an extraordinarily beautiful performance. With some fifty or so dancers it was exquisite, breathtaking. At one point, the male lead does a solo in which the climax of the dance is a series of great leaps in a large circle using the full dimensions of the stage. As he does so, he is some five feet in the air, a feat of not only aesthetic power, but of striking athleticism. I was immediately struck by Marcia's comment. This instance of classical dance was indeed a magnificent attempt to leave the earth.

Two years later we are privileged to see Marcia as dancer and choreographer in a performance of the "Plagues of Egypt." I was intrigued by the difference in the performance and the way in which it did indeed "get back to the earth." For example, in the plague of the flies the auditorium is in black light. Marcia has the dancers, a troupe of about a dozen, in black costumes with illuminated stripes that glow in that special lighting. To top—or should I say "bottom"—it off, the dancers are darting around the stage on their stomachs riding automechanic skeeters to the *zzzz*-sounds of flies. I could not help juxtaposing those spectacular leaps in Moscow with this wonderful presentation of flies, the one "leaving the earth" and the other truly "getting down" on it.

7. Finally, Marcia says that people must be given permission to move. In some churches this will be clearly going against the grain. It may not be done in the traditional services of many congregations, and that's all right. It will usually be necessary to do these innovations in alternative services. Further, we do not know how to do these movements and dances. They will need to be learned. Youth groups, church camps, small groups, experimental efforts, and a host of other opportunities will be needed to develop them. Nevertheless, permission to begin is important. The worship of the future will involve congregational dance. It can be learned and can be a significant way to glorify God. It will, of course, need to be indigenous to the people involved. In my part of the country, for example, the indigenous dances of the Native American tribes have often been excluded from Christian worship, as has been the drum. This is a serious denial of Incarnation in my understanding and underscores the need for worship to take a contextual form.[11]

I maintain that electronic culture is one where at least three processes are characteristic of the ways people so acculturated engage the world today. These processes of imaging, of the percussive use of sound, and visualization are deeply encoded in the concrete lives of electronic generations and contribute to the social construction of who people are. Complex relations are generated among these three processes, and their interaction in spectacles and events in popular culture give them emergent qualities not possessed by any one of them alone. Out of the technological developments that occur and the cultural activities that make use of these, new practices come into play, practices that are formative of the way people sense, feel, think, and know. The focus here is on the practices of spectacle, performance, soul music, and dance. While these are not exhaustive by any means, they are crucial in understanding electronic culture and especially its impact on the lived lives of people today.

Further, these practices are basic to cultural processes of bonding and commitment, matters that do not receive the kind of attention they deserve in assessments of electronic culture. Rather, the comments one typically hears about electronic culture are that it does not generate commitment and bonding, indeed that these are not characteristic of the generations born since World War II. I believe this to be decidedly wrong and arrogant. What has happened instead is that the practices and dynamics of bonding and commitment have changed. The characteristics of these practices and their dynamics thus become increasingly important not only in understanding what is happening but in efforts to change the way things are. These considerations engage us in the next chapter.

CHAPTER SEVEN

Convergence, Experience, Meaning, and Commitment

I was in Ohio dealing with electronic culture and the issues of commitment and bonding. Jacob Golden Jr., a pastor, came over during the break and said, "Tex, you need to work with the Grateful Dead and the Deadheads."

I must have looked at him quizzically because he then said, "You do know who they are, don't you?"

"Well, yes, but why should I be studying them?"

"Because of the commitment they draw from their fans," he explained with a bit of exasperation that I apparently did not know this. "Look, I've been to 150 Grateful Dead concerts."

"Holy cow!" I say, "That's three years of regular church attendance."

"Aw, that's nothing, I know people who've been to three hundred Grateful Dead concerts."

"That's six years of regular church attendance," I thought to myself, but decided then and there that I would follow his advice. I found Linda Kelly's book on the Deadheads, which is basically a compendium of testimonies by Grateful Dead fellow artists, friends, and followers. Her chapter entitled "Getting It" is especially helpful [207–29]. Here the testimonies describe variously the impact of the Dead on people's lives. Of course the music is basic, and the "born again" Deadheads testify to the multisensory nature of the event, to the way it generates self-esteem, encourages creativity, and validates experience [207]. The band strikes a chord "as being something very familiar inside myself" [208], they "kept me interested in alternative

76

styles of living," they encourage experimentation, the band is "an experimenting entity of ever-evolving ideas" [209].

Issues of commitment come through these witnesses. One woman says, "It's about sharing, giving, respecting our fellow humans, animals, everything . . . it's about a way of living" [209–10]. These commitments go beyond the music and the band, she says. It's about a freedom and about living a harmonious and kind life. Deadheads talk about friends, about daily life, about rituals of hugging, and the joyful exuberance of the concerts. One says, "when they play, people just smile." The music is "spiritual," it confirms who people are, it provides a kind of identity, and, to be sure, it is clearly pleasurable and fun.

These testimonies impress me with the fact that the concerts are not reducible to any one thing, not even the music and the band. As one person says, it is "the *whole* experience . . . the scene thing" [217]. Or, in other words, Deadheads describe it as "the community of it all" [221].[1] Timothy Leary, self-described as a chaos engineer, states that "there is a true and, in the best sense of the word, formal, non-hierarchical, nonecclesiastical religion about the Dead" [223].

I see in the Grateful Dead something very important going on that is not the possession of the Dead alone, and certainly in its authenticity, cannot be attributed to electronic media alone, but is an artistic and communal enactment of a basic dynamic of electronic culture.

Experience, Convergence, and Meaning

I am struck when reading academic treatments of electronic culture how often these thinkers write of "reading" media. Media are made to sound like a text. I understand that "reading" is used as a metaphor in these treatments, but I think it is a metaphor that distorts what goes on and is therefore a language inadequate to the description of the practices.

As I read the testimonies of the Deadheads, it is not a reading that makes these events so important. Rather, their comments suggest that a total experience takes place in the response of an audience to the multidimensional character of these electronic events. I am struck by the range of the senses brought into play in these concerts. It is not only the music, or the words, or the charisma of the artist, as important as these obviously are; it is not only the percussive use of light and image and beat; it is not only the behavior of the crowd; it is not only the kinesthetic involvement of the audience moving, dancing, and typically staying on their feet the entire time; it is not only the smells and tastes of the event. It is really all of these and more together. *The power of the event for the participative audience occurs in their convergence of these. The fundamental contribution of the electronic culture is the convergence of these sensory experiences.*

Such concerts are orchestrations of a gestalt and the participants do not merely "read" concerts or "hear" or "view" them. They *converge* them by drawing together the multidimensional setting into a vortex of personal and social yearnings and satisfactions. If, as Marshall McLuhan maintains, electronic media are extensions of the central nervous system and if we are formed, in part, socially by media, then convergence becomes an extraordinary fulfillment of the persons and groups who gather at these spectacles. It is not reducible to crowd behavior alone, though this is important, but rather relates deeply to the social construction of human beings in an electronic culture. It "sings their song" metaphorically in the sense that it pulls together sensory and social codings that have shaped their lives—or "wired"—them and satisfies them in organic experience. That is, when people are socially constructed, encoded, "wired," formed by these practices, and when they then come to a spectacle, they participate in the enactment of an event that brings together not only the performance but the satisfaction of a range of yearnings that constitute who they basically are.

Leonard Sweet speaks to this when he says that the issue is no longer meaning but experience. At the same time, Mark Johns has moved this a further step with his claim that "meaning is conveyed through experience" and that electronic media "store meaning in convergence." He maintains that meaning is a function of the "total electronic experience"; it incorporates sound and the visual as one gestalt. Hence, meaning is not found in words or images or the music alone, "but in the intersection of several of the 'channels' simultaneously." These media carry and store meaning in the "convergences" of this total experience.[2] Quentin Schultze et al. argue for something close to Johns's point. They attempt to "understand the rock phenomenon . . . [and] try to produce a 'gestalt' of the experience and the meaning of rock. These two dimensions are not neatly separable, since it is true of rock—as it is of most art—that *its experience contains its meaning.*"[3]

While Johns's comments are focused on electronic media generally, I would argue that his comments are even more true of spectacle and of the convergence and meaning that occur there. More than this, as I read the testimonies of the Deadheads, they describe an experience that is quite in keeping with this dynamic of convergence. While the label "convergence" is abstract, the dynamic when "thickly described" in terms of spectacle is not.[4]

Meaning and Experience

Still, I am not yet satisfied with the notion of "meaning in experience." It needs more analysis. I came up against this quite personally last year in a conversation with my son. To understand the significance of our conversation you need to know a couple of things. First, our older son was killed in a motorcycle accident. He died of a head injury. You can well imagine that we are apprehensive about such injuries with any of our family.

Second, this is even more complicated by the fact that our other son, Shawn, competes in Shotokan Karate on the national and world levels. He has finished second or third in the nationals several times, though never having won it, and on the world level he finished in the top eight the last two tournaments, but, again, has not won it. But when you finish that high you fight in many matches. He is engaged in serious competition, and at that level you inevitably get hit often and hard. He suffers a broken nose every year, not to mention fractured knuckles and ribs and a lost tooth now and then. Head injury is an ever present possibility.

As parents we worry a lot. Certain kinds of phone calls from Shawn can scare us. Such a call came last summer.

"Hey, Dad, wait till you hear what I did today!" These kinds of comments usually accompany feats that I would not do for the world. They usually come after taking on some challenge of major proportions. He frightens me.

"Oh, Shawn, I'm not sure I want to know."

"Aw, Dad, it was wonderful. I want to get you up in one."

"What are you talking about?"

"Dad, I jumped out of an airplane this afternoon!"

"With a parachute or not?" I wryly asked, because sometimes I believe he could jump out of an airplane without a chute, land on his feet, and not be hurt.

"Aw, come on, Dad, I used a parachute. But, listen, you've got to try it."

"Not on your life!"

"But, Dad, when you jump out of the plane you free-fall for a thousand feet! Have you ever done that?"

"Thank God, NO!"

"Dad, when you fall, the wind is just tearing at your arms and legs and pulling the skin back from your face, and the ground is really coming up at you. It is just incredible."

"Shawn, why would you do that?"

"Listen, Dad, when you open the chute, it pops you pretty hard, but then everything gets quiet. It's so peaceful . . . it's beautiful . . . it's like everything stops . . . and then you kind of smooth down to the ground."

"Shawn, why would you do such a thing?"

"Oh, Dad, there you go again. It's not a 'why' question, it's a 'rush' question."

I've thought a lot about his comment. While we love each other a great deal, we are very different on this issue. I grew up in a cabstand from the time I was in the fifth grade until I went away to college. I began to answer the phone there when I was twelve and could write down addresses and later I started driving when I was sixteen and could get a commercial license. A cabstand is a very strategic place to see the underbelly of a small town. You have to contend with drunks every day, some of whom want to "clean your clock." You take people home on payday who have already blown the week's check. You see the "reputable" people in terribly "compromised" situations. These at the "top" of the community and those on the "bottom" come by all the time. You see violence. You witness the profound ugliness of racism. You relate to people who one day are alive and the next are dead.

The point is that by the time I was in my late teens, I was asking a lot of "why" questions. Why is there so much wrong? Why do people screw up their lives so much? Why is there so much evil in the world? My issue was the problem of evil, though I would not have put this language on it. When I got to college and finally realized that this was a question one dealt with in philosophy, I remember feeling that at last I could work on something that had troubled me all along.

The older I get, the more I realize that understanding things by being able to explain them has become extremely important to me. On some of these matters I was not able to do much about them, perhaps only putting them into words. At least my being able to name them and engage them in terms of "why" questions gave me some sense of having power in relationship to them. I'm trying to say that *meaning in words* became central to my life and is probably why, in part, I have been in an academic institution for over thirty years. This is also deeply related to print culture.

While Shawn has experienced some very difficult times, "why" questions are not his issues. Perhaps it's because he grew up with a father who always pressed such things. Also, he had to go out and *find* experiences while they always seemed to come looking for me. He did not grow up in a place like a cabstand, but certainly he had other kinds of issues, like the drug culture and the sexual revolution, the Vietnam War and the Civil Rights struggle. His experience with so much mendacity in the national life left him looking for something real. I had too much "reality" and a good deal of it was bad. He had too much falsehood and it was distortive and misleading. In these ways he has participated in his generation as I have participated in mine.

The power of electronic culture left its effect as well. If my world—certainly since I began higher education—has been one of theory, conceptualization, and discourse, his has been one engaged through image, sound as beat, and visualization. In these senses he looks for *meaning in experience*. He looks for a rush while I ask why.

Meaning As a Practice

This difference between meaning in words and meaning in experience is an important one. Yet, meaning can be a vacuous notion. What does meaning mean? It is a rather useless abstraction unless one can name the practices in which it is embedded. With this in mind it will be helpful to look at the practices in which I use it and the contrasting ways Shawn does. This difference is shared widely in contemporary

81

culture.[5] Twelve percent of adults are "thrill-seekers" according to SRI International of Menlo Park, California.[6] In the Values and Life Styles 2 demographic program, these researchers found that Experiencers made up one of eight lifestyle groups in the U.S. This group seems to be growing, especially with the Generation X crowd, but lacks no participation from Boomers like our son.[7] A recent news report indicates that "extreme sports" continue to grow in the U.S.[8]

In my case, I engage in practices of observing and thinking. I am especially interested in attempting to describe and explain a series of problems I have confronted over and over again in my life. I want to be able to re-present in words as carefully as I can what makes up the circumstances that have led to so much pain and suffering for people I see around me and in the larger world. Hence, I am very interested in the semantics of words and in attempting to use them as accurately as I can to say what is going on. Moreover, my approach is rational and analytical, and I am engaged in an explicit exploration of these problems in the hope of being able to articulate them well enough that others will say, "That makes sense to me." This practice takes seriously knowledge as a discipline.

In Shawn's case, he is seeking in the parachute jump an emotive high, a rush. He is not attempting to explain but to embody. I think here especially of the difference between the way we express our different practices. I may say of someone's argument that "it is a compelling statement of a position." Shawn would say of his experience that it is "cool" or "fantastic." Where I want to explain, he wants to exclaim. Where I am rational, he is nonrational. If I want to re-present in words, he wants to present in an enactment. If I want to name the dynamics of grief and loss, he wants to weep. If I want to articulate the dynamics of humor, he wants to laugh. My search for meaning is in discourse that can withstand debate and counterargument. His search is in an emotive and embodied excitement that can claim an undeniable authenticity. My approach has the "distance" of a print culture; his has the "convergence" of an electronic one.

The following chart attempts to summarize these differences. The chart is an example of the way *I* would do such things, and *not* as Shawn would!

Meaning as a Practice

In Words	*In Experience*
Descriptive	Emotive
Explanatory	Embodied
Re-presentational	Presentational
Discourse	Vernacular
Rational	Nonrational
Analytical	Experiential
Explicit exploration	Implicit seeking
Verifiable "truth"	Subjective "truth"
Knowing as a discipline	Knowing as lived
Observational distance	Intimate immersion

Obviously, there is at least one problem with this kind of polar description. Such schemes leave out the middle ground between us where our lives are practiced. It is certainly not my intention to say that I never experience or that Shawn never thinks! Nevertheless, the polar distinction is an attempt to unpack the difference between meaning in words and meaning in experience as practices, and what is a significant difference between us even if it is not an absolute one.

Spectacle and Convergence

Spectacle, with the combination of performance, soul music, and dance, provides the quintessential experience where convergence is the basic practice and the dynamic that generates participation and meaning. In describing convergence this way, however, I am not suggesting meaning that only is experienced in one's head.

First, convergence is a cognitive dynamic. While it takes on the character of aesthetic cognition, it is nonetheless a knowing. Partly this comes from the music itself, not only because sound conveys meaning in Ong's sense, but because meaning in music, as we see above, provides the basic narrative for many people's lives. Surely the great majority of those who go to particular concerts do so because these musicians play their soul music. But it also is a knowing through the use of light and visualization. Again, visualization provides authenticity for many younger people today, and, when light imitates sound, visualization participates in the dynamics of the aural and their contemporary capacities to create intimacy and meaning. Yet, it is actually the whole experience that is a knowing and, while we can point to dimensions of the music and the visualization, these, as important as they are, do not exhaust the experience and the convergence of it. It is cognitive, but it is a multisensory and embodied knowing. It is heard, seen, sung, danced, touched, tasted, and smelled.

Second, this knowing, especially in a narrative form, is a source of identity. Simon Frith, the British rock critic says it well: "Music constructs our sense of identity through the experiences it offers of the body, time, and sociability, experiences which enable us to place ourselves in imaginative cultural narratives."[9] Frith points out that "identity is necessarily a matter of ritual," and that self-identity *is* cultural identity. He understands that one's subjectivity is imputed from the larger social and cultural environment around us, and that the repetitive practice of ritual is a principal means by which we take on culture. From this point of view the spectacle is a basic ritual of contemporary life and central to the identity of its practitioners.[10]

Third, spectacle develops emotional bonds and an intensive inner sense of being a part of something much bigger than oneself alone. It can be an utterly captivating event giving one a sense of unity with many others. It is worth reiterating Durkheim's insight that when you get people in close physical proximity, focus their attention on a common object, and engage them in exercises that arouse emotion, bonding occurs. In this sense, whom we gather with will determine whom we are bonded with.

Fourth, spectacle both articulates and enacts the lives of those gathered. That is, it not only *reflects* the lives of the people so gathered by the playing of their soul music and the uses of significant conventions to "tell their stories" and "sing their songs," but it also *enacts* those lives. A dramatization occurs in which the participants construct not a reality that *"stands behind"* what they are doing but ritualizes a reality that is *within* it.[11] It ritualizes the relations people esteem and yearn for in their lives. In convergence, spectacle claims and reclaims the stories that the music recalls and, at the same time, "retells" in the "real presence" of those gathered.

Finally, though not exhaustively, spectacle generates commitments and convictions. The reduction of spectacle to entertainment, to an idle and passive consumption of amusement, is to miss the power of ritualized behavior. Surely there are amusements in spectacle form that have no enduring significance, but these are not of the kind addressed here in which basic indigenous practices of electronic culture stimulate the encodings of people wired to its charges, events in which people find not only their lives reflected but dramatically enacted in identity and deep emotional bonding to others. To claim spectacle as generative of commitments and convictions does not by any means suggest that these are righteous or good. And I do not mean to restrict such commitments and convictions to those like the Deadheads alone. Spectacles bring out lifestyle commitments, the conviction to live out the story condensed in the narratives of the music, made authentic in the sight and visualization, and kinesthetically embodied in dance. Such rituals are the stuff of which forms of identity and character are made.

Electronic culture can be characterized in terms of engaging the world through image, sound as beat, and visualization with all three of these understood in terms of the shape they have taken especially in the last fifty years. These have powerfully affected Boomers, Xers, and now Millenials. Out of a social, economic, and cultural milieu where image, beat, and visualization have become so important, certain indigenous practices form. The focus here is especially on the practice of spectacle and its role in popular culture and popular music concerts. Other basic practices are integrated into spectacle, especially the practices of performance, soul music, and dance.

Amidst these multisensory and highly participative practices a central dynamic of convergence is the means by which an array of experience is taken in by participants. This dynamic is basic to the conveyance of meaning in experience and, indeed, in the "storage" of meaning, with meaning understood as a practice. Moreover, spectacle when so constituted is a basic practice of knowing, identity, and bonding; is used in reflecting and enacting the lives of its participants; and is an outward sign of conviction and commitment. I believe it is one of the single most powerful practices operating in this way for the great majority of the youngest three generations in the United States and in a good part of younger people in the larger world.

This, of course, does not mean it is necessarily good or that it is adequate or that it is outright evil. As captivating as spectacle, performance, soul music, and dance can be, they can also be the stuff of captivity. Moreover, Lawrence Grossberg claims that, in the mattering maps of contemporary life, we are in a situation in which what is significant is not important and what is important is not significant.[12] Does this mean that spectacle is finally a lot of sound and fury signifying nothing of great importance? Are we seeing the generation of identities, solidarities, lives, and commitments that don't mean anything and don't amount to much? Is it all vanity, as Qoheleth, The Preacher, warned (Eccl. 2:1)?

More specifically, we need to turn more directly to these questions as they confront the church. How does it discern its role in electronic culture? The church must always engage the culture of which it is a part. As important as it is for the church to be a culture in its own life, it is also inevitably a participant in a wider culture.

Further, I have put off as long as I can a critique of electronic culture. It is now necessary not only to look at what is wrong but to see if there is any way electronic culture offers its own forms of critique.

CHAPTER EIGHT

Spectacle, Story, and Community

A growing body of criticism is devoted to electronic culture. It focuses on a range of matters from concerns like Baudrillard's about the artificial world of images masquerading reality to a mounting apprehension about the disembodied character of virtual life. Increasingly the couch potato is rivaled by the info junkie. People worry that the Internet and cybercommunity will replace face-to-face interaction of actual people occupying the same physical space. Moreover, a new set of injuries arise with the coming of the computer, such as repetitive strain injuries or RSI. We worry about the impact of television and computers on our children. Increasing numbers of parents and other adults raise questions about the easy access of pornography via computer or cable dishes. The bilging diet of violence does affect children, but the makers of TV shows, movies, and much popular music seem unconcerned, rather claiming some "right" to do what they do in pursuit of profit, seemingly more concerned about making statements denying their culpability than in focusing on the type of product they promote. Concerns are also raised about images of gender, race, and class, and the defining and distorting impact of these images in our social lives.

Others grow restive with the extraordinary threat of surveillance offered through electronic culture whether through the Internet or through the information processing that computers make possible in their analysis of credit card data, demographic studies, and the selling of customer lists and purchases. We fear big government and the transnational corporations that have a corner on the ownership, use, and sweep of this new technology. Hence, the issue of control and power is a constant focus of the debate, as is the sense that electronic culture is the servant of a consumerist capitalism that commodifies life and turns some people increasingly into buyers and debtors riven with a neomania to seek ever-new thrills from the latest offerings of an economy less and less concerned with need and more and more with generating wants as necessities.

In the midst of this a growing inequality goes on apace in what some have called "the race to the bottom." The elites tell us it is because we must move out onto the stage of a global economy and that sacrifice must be made. Yet, it seems that it is the bottom two-thirds that must sacrifice as the elites and others at the top receive unprecedented rewards for their "leadership."

People who love peace see in electronic culture a new kind of conflict such as the Gulf War with its visual proximity but psychological distance, its antiseptic death (smart bombs), and our intoxication with media and high-tech weaponry.[1]

This is a short list and certainly more than I can take on here. My focus, though, has been on spectacle as it occurs in popular culture and especially popular music concerts. This is a basic and indigenous practice in electronic culture along with component practices of performance, soul music, and dance. It is a formative set of practices and participates significantly in the "rewiring" occurring in our culture.

In this chapter my concern is to critique spectacle and to raise substantive questions about it. I intend to do so from a perspective I call prophetic faith. That is, I want to raise issues from the position of one who stands in the Christian community with its commitment to the reign of God. In this stance the story of the world is seen within the story of God's work in Christ and God's ongoing action in the world through the Spirit. In this story, reality is covenantal where justice draws its makeup from the character of covenantal relationships and where peace is the ultimate consummation and aim of the world. This means that the church has an active role to play in building its life together, as a people committed to a covenantal, just, and peaceable reign.

Hence I discuss spectacle in terms of three issues. The first is the question of story or tradition. What story informs spectacle? The second is that of community. Does spectacle generate community? What would it mean for spectacles to be in the service of community? And a third and crucial question for our purposes is that of what resources electronic culture and spectacle specifically bring to the question of critique. Many critics argue that electronic culture offers no serious resources for doing analysis and critical engagement of the issues facing the larger society. I want to challenge this and to suggest emergent and indigenous practices that do indeed perform critical functions. But first, we turn to the pivotal issue of story.

Spectacle and Story

The first of these issues has to do with the question of tradition and story, two terms I will use interchangeably. We have already learned from Ruth Finnegan that popular music provides the convincing narratives for most people's lives and that in the context of a spectacle, these narratives in image, beat, and visualization take on intensity, bonding, life, commitment, and conviction. This is powerful stuff. Even more so than it seems on a first hearing because I am convinced that life and thought are mediated by story. It is through the story of our lives that we come to understand ourselves. We discover that we are historical beings, that our lives truly are contingent. It is through story that we realize how much history constitutes who we are and how fateful our practices are in the contingent and socially constructed character of our lives.[2] So to say that spectacle tells a story is to move into fateful territory.

But there's the bite. Which story or tradition informs spectacle? Particularly in our time of large spectacles, is there any story that can or does inform spectacle? Does it become simply the constitution of a large group of fans or the short-lived, shared consciousness of a few hours? Does it simply create the appearance of a bonding? Does it have any enduring value except as entertainment? Are the Deadheads and other "true believers" like them the exception to a much larger group of people for whom spectacle is an emotional binge and an entertainment high? Or are the stories so disparate that as significant as they are, they do not bond to much past the moment? Perhaps there's a better way to say it: Does spectacle need a compelling story to do its best work?

I think here of the place of tradition. Most people today seem to be anti-traditional. Tradition is understood as mired in the past, as a straitjacket of conformity to rules and procedures and to beliefs and values no longer relevant to contemporary life. Views like these fail to see how much life and thought are dependent on a tradition.

The anti-tradition stance is often a facade for a "tradition," and quite an anemic one at that. I think here particularly of the degree to which consumerism has become a tradition in the United States: the continual interest in choices, the fetish for the new, the moral justification of questions like "Well, what's wrong with it?" or "Don't I have a right to do it?" None of these raise the question of the nature of the good served by such conduct, although a good is often assumed in the claims. That is, individual choice and the pursuit of privatistic interests are the good, and the expectation is that they are to be honored as such.

As I say, this is a tradition, but one difficult to justify once its specific claims and commitments are made explicit. For example, can one really argue that individual choice is an automatic good? Does the choice itself have anything to do with the quality and intrinsic claim of an action? Does the claim that one has a right to do something justify it morally? Surely one can admit that human agency needs to be sustained without falling into a position in which one's individual choice encompasses the good in some mindless attempt to satisfy the incessant urges of a consumerist fanaticism.

I think here of the kind of spiritual "hopscotch" people play with world religions. Some people, for example, choose some fascinating aspect of different faith commitments and "adopt" it as a part of their "cosmopolitan spirituality." As they say, "taking the best of all the religions and choosing my own." Using this approach they may "pick up" in hopscotch fashion a "piece" each from Zen, Christianity, Judaism, Islam, or New Age. Wade Clark Roof has described this as multilayered spirituality.[3] Typically these "cosmopolitan spiritualities" are exercises in mere belief, that is, taking some series of ideas that are appealing and used to shore up their consumerist subjectivity.[4] When challenged, one finds that these devotees usually do not know much about these various religious practices and certainly do not engage them much more than they do in choosing the brands of cat food they purchase for their feline accessories. Take Zen, for example. I often find people who "adopt" continually some belief in meditation—sporadically used, *maybe*—and claim it for their own, displaying it in conversation but not devoting themselves to it. In radical contrast, Zen monks spend a lifetime *practicing* such meditation. The practices of these monks are forms of knowing and of shaping life, feeling and thought that forever lie beyond the grocery bag of beliefs taken home to fill the shelves of subjectivity in a closet of inexpensive finds from the sales tables of America's psychic department stores. These items of spirituality take their place on these shelves right next to a running fashion of pop psychologies with the low-fat, low-calorie ingredients of transactional analysis, Myers-Briggs, and family systems theory.

Well, what's wrong with it? Apart from the reduction of ultimate commitments to mere belief, apart from the trivialization of a rich religious tradition, apart from an imperial and colonial grabbing up of abstract notions from the verdant land of a religious history, nothing much is wrong. Except this: Consumerist spiritualities do not fill or satisfy the human heart any more than do other commercial purchases driven by the emptiness of a commodity culture.

"Don't we have a right to do it?" Certainly it would not do to make a law or form social policy to attempt to prevent it. But does it ever more need exposure. These spiritualities reflect the turn toward subjectivity in journey spirituality and away from a practice-based journeying of the spirit in concrete lived life. The practices of these spiritualities are sporadic and extrinsic. They are bereft of a great story. They are the worst of a consumerist tradition parading in the guise of an ultimate conviction. Their individualism lacks the accountability and the formative power of a corporate community. Their privatism shrinks from the public arena and makes peripheral the most important commitments of human existence. They are not meant to propel one into mission but are procured for individual use.

Without a compelling story, spectacle can readily become a ritualized cult of individualistic and consumerist "tradition." It becomes a bonding to choices and "feel good" experience. It delivers serial commitment to recurring rendezvous in which one brings an individualistically conceived story, privately appropriated and publicly celebrated.

Those who attend such popular spectacles are not necessarily cultural nitwits who do not have a clue about what they are doing. I am not generally considered a snarling, huffy, moralist who just can't stand fun and pleasure. It is rather that popular music, augmented in the power of spectacle, does provide the convincing narratives of most people's lives. The question then becomes crucial as to what that story is. In the anti-traditionalism of the culture, in the privatism, individualism, and consumerism that insinuate themselves into so much of our lives, in the power of spectacle to bond and establish commitment, we

91

have a practice that requires a vigilance about its impact. Central to that vigilance is the question of which story, or whose story, is at work.

Spectacle and Community

In the bonding and commitment of spectacle the question of community inevitably arises. Whom you gather with determines to whom you will be bonded. We are the company we keep. This not only raises the question of the story that informs the event, it also raises the matter of the kind of relationships induced by that event, because the character of the gathering will determine the nature of the relationships.

Spectacles tend to create publics, not communities. The reasons why seem apparent. Typically they do not provide a common story but rather people bring their stories with them and seem to make their own uses of them. Even Deadheads are quite various in their appropriation of the Dead concerts. Further, there are not usually the ongoing ties of a community in which people share a broader range of life together. This is one reason why spectacles can be distortive and harmful. People can be "taken in" by the legitimating power of a spectacle. They can become the kind of public that will support some larger societal action, but still not be engaged in that action on the kind of basis that offers a clear-eyed view of what is going on.

Hence, what kind of public is generated by spectacle? What kind of legitimating effort is being made? Again, people can resist spectacles and use them to their own ends, but they can also be swept up in the power of them.

Perhaps yet another question at this point is that of whether one is engaged in still other spectacles that counter or resist or subvert spectacles of a distortive or destructive kind. I contend that we need, at the least, alternative spectacles. More than that, we need spectacles that oppose and subvert many of those of the larger society. We need a radically different story and community, not merely publics, if we are to be sustained by commitments to goods that question the consumerism, the individualism, the violence, the worship of winning, the commitments to war as redemptive, and the rest.

Let it be clear that such a story and community will engage an electronic culture for the foreseeable future. It will not do to turn away

92

from this emergent culture, which is now not only shaping the external world but fashioning our senses, our feelings, our forms of reason, and our knowing.

In the church we confront a situation perhaps even more fateful than the one Martin Luther faced in the coming of the printing press. He caught a glimpse of the enormous implications of the shifts that it would bring. He knew that the church would have to make use of this transformative development in the West. In a very real sense Protestantism is a tradition born of the printed word. While one should not be uncritical of this tradition in its support of modernity and its accommodation to a rising bourgeois class, one should also not be inattentive to the faithfulness of the people of the story who met the challenges of their time.

Our relation to God is always mediated by culture and history. This has been true from the beginning. The apostle Paul knew that the forms of commitment that drew the people in the Jerusalem church would not address the gentile world. Perhaps the ugliest conflict in the first-century church grew out of Paul's move toward a different contextualization of the faith.

The story of church history can be read as a move from one cultural context to another, with each context requiring a renewed mobilization of the church's life and thought to engage new social forms. The radically different paths taken by the Roman and the Eastern Orthodox churches reflect, in part, the very different cultures they confronted. Today, the mission of the church, say, in Africa, South America, and Asia looks quite different from that in Europe and North America. So far as we can tell, it will always be so.

At the same time, the church is not to be in conformity to the world.[5] If we are to be all things to all people, it is for the sake of the gospel.[6] Our task is one of being transformed by the ongoing work of the Spirit. The church always has a critical and prophetic role to play that is of the very essence of its life as a faithful people before God who live their lives in the hope of the reign of God.

But this, too, takes on a cultural form. For example, in the Gospels of Matthew, Mark, and Luke Jesus comes teaching in parables. His teaching takes on the character of an oral culture. Paul's writing is done in a discursive style. His writing in Romans, for example, fits well with his literate training, although the printing press is a millenium and a half away.

Oral, Literate, and Electronic "Critique"

It is my contention that critique takes different forms in an oral and literate culture and is taking a different form in electronic culture. For example, in an oral culture "critique" will often come in the form of a series of stories punctuated with sayings and proverbs that may not make any sense until one comes to the very end. Only then do you know that you have been handed your head in your hands. Moreover, in oral culture, contradiction and inconsistency may not be important. Some oral cultures do not even pay attention to contradiction. The language for "critique" in oral culture captures something of its character in a vernacular that suggests its difference from literate critique: "She put him in his place," "Telling it like it is," "He straightened him out," "We had a 'come to Jesus talk,' " "She made it plain," "He set her down." Such common expressions tell us a good deal about the character of oral "critique."

In contrast, literate culture focuses on analysis and looks carefully for inconsistency and contradiction. It is committed to conceptually precise, comprehensive, and coherent propositional claims. It is done in anticipation of critical responses and attempts to defend its position against intellectual attack. Yet, more recent criticism raises questions with literate approaches. One view contends that reason and critique prove to be deeply conditioned by tradition. Another argues that literality presumes metaphors that may provide disclosure, on the one hand, but obscure a state of affairs, on the other. Still another position maintains that the use of a text promotes the power and interests of certain groups and defends class interests. Yet other critics argue that meaning cannot be pinned down by language. Such approaches raise sharp questions with literate critique, even as critics make use of such critique when they point out its relativity.[7]

I think critique is basically a literate practice as we understand it. For this reason I put the word in quotes when using it with oral and electronic culture. Still, both oral and electronic cultures know how to raise questions and to indicate that the "fish stink." In spite of the arguments that electronic culture cannot do critique, I contend that electronic media can, indeed, do so provided one does not require that it be done in literate form. It is also quite clear that such "critique" is desperately needed in the emerging culture of electronic media. There is more than enough wrong to keep such "criticism" busy.

94

CHAPTER NINE

Electronic Critique

So far as I can tell there are no "universal" characteristics of electronic "critique." Nor are my comments, to be sure, the last word about these practices. Rather, I name a few "critical" practices that are in use in electronic culture. The future portends an immense reservoir of critique. The resources of digitalization and virtual reality are without limit in human terms, provided access to them can be broadly shared, a provision by no means guaranteed by present institutional arrangements.

So this beginning is a statement of practices that offers genuine opportunities for the church and other groups concerned about a common good. These practices also are aimed primarily at the spectacle as a means of alternative, oppositional, and subversive forms of life.

The first form of electronic critique relates to the matter of ecological fit. I have described above the kind of gestalt that is generated in electronic culture in terms of image, beat, and visualization. Further, the practices of spectacle, performance, soul music, and dance offer a multisensory, kinesthetic narrative that is a basic source of bonding and commitment. And, finally, the dynamic of convergence is the means by which meaning is conveyed and bonding and commitment condensed and appropriated by participants. When all these things come together in a holistic engagement, they take on the character of an ecology. It is an environment.

As an ecology, spectacle requires fit. The very character of such an environment has a holistic lure toward union, toward things coming together, toward things being together. The other side of this requirement is that lack of fit is dramatic and stunning, in the same way that a literary metaphor juxtaposes contradictory images. There may be no more graphic way of doing critique.

I think here of the video of Louis Armstrong singing "What a Wonderful World," a beautiful and expressive popular song filled with a sensitive gratitude for the world, its beauty, its people, the sheer exhilaration of being alive. However, as Armstrong sings, the video depicts the most despicable acts of human hatred, the violation of earth, air and water, and of war and the destruction of life and hope. Clearly, the pictures do not fit; they are wrong; the world is meant to be different. I do realize that there can be more than one convergence of this video. One can conclude that the world is not wonderful and that the song is a farce. While I believe that this is the conclusion of the few and not the many, nevertheless it points out the importance of the story and the community of those who receive it, once again crucial factors in the "critique" of electronic media and its participants.

The second form of electronic critique, and closely related to the above, is that of the place of aesthetics in electronic "critique." The juxtaposition of the beautiful and the repugnant are compelling forms of presentation. The beauty of the world and its people and the way we ravish the world, violate others, and betray ourselves are stunning indictments of the ugliness that so befoul the intricate relationships and destiny we share.

Third, the various uses of images can be penetrating forms of electronic "critique." I think here specifically of the use of a riveting image, one so compelling that it "tells" an unforgettable story almost by itself. Remember the picture of the little girl running down the road in Vietnam, naked and crying? It seems to capture all the hurt and death of that dreadful war. I find even now that I cannot get that image out of my mind. The amazing power of the photograph—I remember also a video—in an electronic culture is that it does not move! In my viewing of the photograph it bespeaks the obdurate persistence of evil in that conflict. Not only can I not forget it, I do not want to forget it. I want to be continually reminded of the cost, of the incalculable suffering, and of the necessity of not allowing a drift into that kind of quagmire and destruction again.[1]

Images can also be sequenced and juxtaposed in "critique." The motion picture *Dead Man Walking* provides a telling example. The motion picture is the story about one of two men who come upon a couple kissing on a wooded road. They force the couple from the car and take them deeper into the woods where they rape her and then kill them both. Later caught, the youngest of the two men (Foxworth)

96

awaits execution while seeking a retrial, which is denied shortly before he is executed. During this time a nun develops a pastoral relationship with him and works to help him see the depth of the evil he has done, a recognition he will not accept since he claims a fake innocence of the young man's murder throughout most of the film. In the brief time before his execution, and through the assistance of her ministry, he comes to acknowledge the guilt of his horrific act.

I must say I did not want to go to see the motion picture. I oppose the death penalty under all circumstances and I knew that my sentiments were shared basically by the makers of the movie and that I would only be "rehearsing" my own views by means of it. I went because Peggy wanted to go. I am glad to say I was surprised by the film.

In the execution scene Foxworth is brought in and belted to a gurney. The gurney has appendages that come out and his arms are strapped down to these as well. I am struck by the utter hygienic setting of the execution. He is clean, the room is spotless, everything is in order. He is in house slippers and has been given an antihistamine, the latter in case he is allergic to the poison to be administered. He is told allergic reactions "get messy." It is a modicum of order. Voices maintain a professional, matter-of-fact tone and measure. His arm is rubbed down before the needle is put in place, ostensibly to prevent "infection." Then the needle is inserted, and the tube is connected to the needle.

When he is secured, he is then lifted up before a window to the adjoining room wherein sit the murdered couple's families, the nun, and his lawyer. As he is lifted he is a distorted picture of crucifixion since the gurney and its appendages form a cross, but the appendages of the gurney hang down at about a forty-five degree angle, suggesting, I surmise, that it is a crucifixion, but not one of an innocent man.

Asked if he wants to speak any last words, he says he does. He speaks first to the father of the young man since he personally shot his son: "I don't want to leave this world with any hate in my heart. I want to ask for your forgiveness for what I done. It was a terrible thing I done to take your son away." Then, to the father and mother of the woman, he calls them by name and says: "I hope my death gives you some relief." He then concludes his comments, which are perhaps the summary of the motion picture and the scene: "I just want to say that killing is wrong no matter who does it, whether it's me or y'all or your government."

As the gurney is lowered back and the hour of the execution comes, the switch is thrown to begin the transmission of the poison. With this the scene shifts from the execution to a flashback to the scene of the rape and murders. On the muddy ground of a wooded area the young woman's clothes are stripped away and she lies helpless. The rapists giggle with the delight of demons. I am reminded of hyenas tearing at the flesh of prey yet to die, lost in the passion and violence of ravishing appetites. One can only hear the woman's muffled cries begging them for release underneath their maniacal laughter and monstrous insensitivity to her suffering. One man finishes with her as the other guards her boyfriend, who is pushed face-first to the ground and held at gunpoint.

Suddenly we are back at the execution and the fluid begins its movement through a clear plastic tube, hence visible to the condemned man and to those gathered.

Again, the scene shifts back to the woods. As they once more take turns with the young woman, the older of the two begins to stab her multiple times, and Foxworth shoots her boyfriend in the back of the head.

Back now to the execution scene, Foxworth loses consciousness and his head turns in death.

Then at the scene of the rape and murder we see the young woman crawling toward her boyfriend's dead body. Then she, too, is shot in the back of the head. The two men then leave the scene of the crime and the camera looks down on this opening in the woods from a perspective above. We see the nude body of the young woman and the clothed boyfriend lying facedown in death. Meanwhile at the execution, Foxworth's eyes pop open in the glintless stare of death, and the camera moves to a perspective above him.

I don't know when I have ever seen two wrongs so clearly presented and so strikingly juxtaposed. The execution and the rape and murder scene so closely coincide that they become two executions, not equally wrong, but wrong. The two scenes are polarities. One is dirty, muddy, maniacal, monstrous, and filled with murderous sounds of demonic delight and festive defilement and violation. The other is rational, methodical, careful, hygienic, quiet, with opportunity for last words, and with a lethal silence in the coming of death. In the one they lie facedown; in the other he lies face up. All three are killed.

I left that theater utterly convinced of two things: that rape and murder must end and that I would do more than just feel that way, and that the death penalty must be opposed and that I would do much more than I had. As a result I became more active in letter writing and telephoning my congressional and state representatives and the governor about cases on death row. I also became more disciplined about references to rape and sexual violence in my teaching and speaking, and I have made a point of using this motion picture as an illustration in my lectures on electronic culture in the hope that it would not only illustrate my points about electronic culture but also have an impact on the listeners as it had on me. It clearly affected me.

Further, that motion picture is the most powerful critique I have ever seen. I have never before witnessed the juxtaposition and sequencing of images and story line used with such power. This film demonstrates the capacity of electronic culture and of images and visualization to do the dramatic critique that is said to be impossible by so many of the critics of electronic spectacle.

Fourth, the juxtaposing of sound, and of sound with images and visualization should not be missed. If popular music does provide the convincing narratives for most people's lives, then it is obviously important to address people not only in terms of these narratives, but it may also be necessary to do critique with and against these narratives. The use of counterimages may play a very important role in electronic "critique."

One of my students, Annalise Fonza, demonstrated a competent use of "critique" with respect to some rap music that troubles her. Two songs are particularly of concern: "My Pony" and "No Fake Ones." While Annalise likes rap music very much, she knows that one has to be critical of it as with anything else.

When she asked the young African American teenagers who liked the songs why they liked them, given what the words say, they told her that they did not listen to the words. Apparently, they liked the percussive character of the language rather than its semantics. Nevertheless, Annalise wanted to raise their sensitivity about the music they listen to. So she got the lyrics and had a meeting with the young women. She asked them to listen and watch the songs performed while paying attention to the lyrics. She also asked that they ask themselves several questions about the songs. One of the questions was: How are you honored in the song?

She then made a pivotal move. She did not begin the discussion by asking them what they thought, but rather asked that they first draw a picture of their response to each song in light of her question of how the song honors them.

"My Pony" is a song in which a man invites women to "come ride me." "No Fake Ones" is a song in which the singer labels a woman a "fake one" if she does not provide oral sex. Annalise reported that the pictures the young women drew were "heavy." She says they would not do for publication. They were graphic in their display of body parts and in their indictment of the songs.

Then Annalise made another pivotal move. She did not ask that they then respond in conversation to the song itself, but rather talk about their images. She said it turned out to be one of the best sessions she has ever had with the young women. In discussing their images, they all noted that the singers of the songs did not honor them at all, but were seeking their own gratification without any evident concern for women.

This procedure offers important insight about moving beyond the percussive use of words to the kind of impact they have when given "critical" imaginal attention. Annalise's use of pictures to give young women a role in constructing a response and then the opportunity to discuss their pictures so that they are only indirectly dealing with the semantics of the words is quite helpful for young people who think in images. Annalise asked them to "interpret" the semantics of the words or, perhaps even more important, the narrative of the singers through their pictures, and she used discussion about these in the place of analysis. To be sure, forms of "analysis" and "critique" are done, but not in a literate form of practice. This procedure establishes a questioning of the music even when the beat is good. Moreover, it is a challenge to the narrative of the singer and opens up the alternative, at least, of a different identity for the young women, not one where they are simply tools for the designs of the singer. It is clearly an oppositional practice to the "message" of the songs.

I realize that this is but one of many possible approaches to such music and other aspects of electronic culture. It is meant not as *the* solution to the need for electronic "critique," but as an illustration of its possibilities.

Fifth, Simon Frith names an important way that popular music works as criticism. In reviewing songs like Spoonie Gee's "Spoonin Rap" and "Love Rap" and punk pieces by the early Stones, Kinks, Velvets, Stooges, and Dolls, Frith notes how a song will be first one thing and then another. He notes also how much Black lyrics can embody "jarring emotional juxtapositions." In his analysis of these performers and their music he observes that they "move from *description* to *emotion* to *identity*.[2] For example, Spoonie Gee begins his "Spoonin Rap" with lyrics describing "how cool he is, about how sexy women are; then it's about don't do dope, don't steal, you'll go to jail."[3] Frith then quotes Frank Kogan who states that "listening to Spoonie is like hearing my own feelings."[4] This then, obviously, raises the question of who one is, the issue of one's identity and one's place in this formulation.

This move from description to emotion to identity is a "logic" of "critique" in electronic culture. Description in this case is not that of linear discourse, but rather a more aesthetic one or a narrative one—these two are not mutually exclusive—that displays circumstances that participants readily see as common to their own lives. The power of performance is such that this description can be loaded with feeling. Both the description and the feeling can be sharply juxtaposed, as Frith suggests, but in doing so they also then raise the question of identity. Who am I in this aesthetic framework? What do I do in these emotionally loaded circumstances?

As soon as I read Frith's passage, I recognized immediately what he "means," as least as I understand it. Perhaps I can "unpack" this "logic" for those who don't find Spoonie Gee or punk groups speaking to their experience.

I shall never forget the first time I heard Elvis Presley's "An American Trilogy." The piece begins with a mournful, haunting rendition of "Dixie" that culminates in the familiar words of longing, "look away, look away, look away, Dixie Land."[5]

I have had enormous trouble with the song ever since I became morally sentient. I associate it with the Stars and Bars (the Confederate flag), the Ku Klux Klan, and the long history of slavery, segregation, and racism. I have fought a long time trying to rid myself of the deeply ingrained racism that hangs like atmosphere in the United States and sticks in our gut like cancer. I simply cannot sing the song in some happy or celebrative way.

So when Elvis begins to sing it in this mournful mood suggesting something of all the hurt and lost life of the South, it floors me. All the contradictions of being a southerner seem to come to the surface, not so much stated but felt. I can sense my love of the South: cool creek bottoms where pea gravel is swept along by a current running through pine trees and sweet gums; I hear a mockingbird at three o'clock in the morning; I lose myself in eight-foot-tall rows of corn and walk out so far that I cannot see anything but the rich green of the stalks; I eat watermelon in the field; feast on crowder peas and cornbread and drink sweetened ice tea; listen to the storytellers at a funeral or down at the fire station; know a "thousand" characters who seem to populate the South the way bitter weed does pasture; watch the land cleaning of a cloudburst with lightning that seems to strike from the earth to an infinite sky. In heart, belly, body, and mind I know I am a southerner, yea a Mississippian, from the sandy gulf, to the piney hills, to the Delta, to the lakes of the northeast, and the big muddy that forms our spine.

Then Elvis shifts to "Hush, little baby, don't you cry, you know your daddy's bound to die," ending the verse with the simple statement that all these trials will soon end. As Elvis sings, I see a Black man being pistol-whipped by a policeman from a time when I was six years old, I hear again the story of a Black man who, falsely accused of raping a White woman, was tied to the rear bumper of a car and dragged through the streets of town until he died. I remember Fannie Rogers, a domestic, whose fingers were constantly infected from an allergy to dishwater, which she could avoid as easily as she could the turning of night and day. And I remember poor and working White people held in place by their loyalty to the South and to the "comfort" that they were, at least, not Black.

There is an enormous sadness about being a southerner. Partly it has to do with what we could have been. Without the racism, the classism, the sexism, we could have really been something. No, I'm not arguing for a supremacist view here, rather that we could have really been something in our own right. With so much going for us how did we mess up so?

These are the descriptions Elvis evokes in me and I am lost in loving a region with a history of towering hate and wrong. Not that the North is morally superior. I've been in the North long enough to know the depth of its evil. It is a highly competent rival to the South in its capacity for injustice.

Lost in these thick memories I am overwhelmed emotionally. I'm in a place where I simply do not want to break down and weep, but I wish I were alone to do so.

Then Elvis moves to "The Battle Hymn of the Republic." I know it is a call to war and invokes the name of Christ to support it. Yet, Elvis does not use those lines. Rather the trilogy ends with "Glory, glory, hallelujah! His truth is marching on!" I am by now struggling with the question of my own identity as a southerner, an American, and a Christian. I feel it deeply but I am forced to consider where I stand.

Looking back I sense how much I was moved by the "logic" that Frith names, when moving from description to feeling to identity. I realize that my reception of the song is specific to me in many ways, but I am also convinced that such hearings of it can be influenced significantly by the setting, the community, and the story in which such "critique" takes place. What I don't doubt is that Frith has named a significant form of electronic "critique."

To sum up, electronic culture is not without its forms of critique. As we see in Chapter 8, story and community are basic in how spectacle is converged. Furthermore, in this chapter we see that other practices of "critique" are forming with the coming of electronic culture. These practices operate more broadly than spectacle only, but they are quite operable in this basic practice as well. The ones we focus on are: the place of ecological fit in electronic culture and its power to display something as unfit, inappropriate, and wrong; aesthetic critique and its capacity to characterize situations as beautiful or repugnant; the sequencing and juxtaposition of images and counterstories to challenge dominant narratives, and a move in popular music that goes from description to emotive feeling to identity in the face of such issues. These are not exhaustive, as I say, but these suggest that electronic culture generally and spectacle specifically are not without "critical" powers.

Such practices of "critique" become desperately important for the church if it is to be in, but not of, the world, if it is to be transformative and not merely conformative, if it is to be all things to all people for the sake of the gospel. It is not faithful simply to accommodate to electronic culture and its offerings, or to any other cultural formation, including a print one. At the same time, it has an important job to do in pitching tent with electronic culture. We face a new situation in that human beings are now being restructured in their senses, feeling, knowing, and reasoning. New practices of bonding and commitment are at work.

A prophetic church of good news will pitch tent with these emergent formations and practices. But it will also bring its own story, its tradition and its distinctive practices to bear. The church lives in a culture but it also *is* a culture.[6] The question is one of how it lives out a faithful life in an electronic world. It is a question of pitching tent with a culture but also of being true to its story.

I know of no range of practices where it is more crucial to be culturally tented and faithfully Christian than in worship. Worship is now the major entry point for people into the faith. In terms of my focus, it is the practice in the church closest to spectacle, though I'll admit that more often than not it does not show it. Worship is one of the most, if not *the* most, crucial practice of bonding and commitment in the church. And most important, it is the place where the community of faith gathers to rehearse The Story and to glorify God. My argument so far must put itself to the test of its appropriateness for Christian worship. If the things I have said have no relation to faithful worship, if I cannot demonstrate that electronic culture can be placed in God's story, I have failed. In the next chapter I must "fish or cut bait," or, in a metaphor closer to the culture under consideration, "display or delete."

CHAPTER TEN

Spectacle As Worship

Usually when one writes a book like this about contemporary life, the next step is to begin talking about *relevant* worship. Recently, I have come to be very suspicious of the word *relevant*, which I suppose is unfair to the word. But I think this emphasis on the word *relevance* comes out of a time in the West when people got their ideas together and then had to find out how they could be used, that is, how they were relevant. I distrust thinking that is abstracted from practices.

The issue is not relevance as far as the church is concerned. The issue is Incarnation. When so-called "traditional" churches are out of touch with the people who live around them, the problem is not that they are irrelevant, but that they not Incarnational.

The most important teaching in Scripture on the Incarnation comes in the first chapter of the Gospel of John where it says "the Word became flesh and lived among us" (v. 14). The word *lived* is an English translation of the Greek word *skēnoō*, which literally means "pitched tent," that is, that the Word became flesh and "pitched tent" *with us.*[1] I understand this as God becoming flesh and joining the indigenous practices of the culture of Jesus' time. Incarnation, therefore, involves three things at least: the Word, become flesh, and pitching tent. The absence of any one of these results in something less than Incarnation.

First, I am intrigued by the notion of the Word becoming "flesh." It is especially interesting when one contemplates that our flesh is encoded culturally and historically and that we are socially constructed. It is not my point that this interpretation of flesh is a biblical notion, but rather that it is significant to reflect on in the light of what we are now learning about human social and historical life. Human "nature" is not the same in all times and places. Its flesh takes on different

105

encodings, different organizations of the senses, different content in feelings, different forms of reason and the rest.[2]

Second, in pitching tent the Word joins a basic and indigenous practice of the world of Jesus' time. Every faithful attempt to be Incarnational requires this kind of indigenous engagement. In the Incarnation God tents with us, tabernacles with us. Such engagement with the world is basic to the Christian faith.

This does not mean, however, that the church pitches tent with *every* practice in a culture. Some are clearly in violation of the faith. I don't care if orgies are indigenous and "work," they are not faithful to the covenantal character of Christian life. But it also means that the church is not to be captive to a range of cultural practices from one culture that it imposes in colonial fashion on another culture because the church has come to identify those as essential to the faith, when they are basically an expression of pitching tent in another and quite different culture.

This position has several important implications. The first has to do with story. Incarnation does not mean that God joins the human story and becomes part of it. Rather Incarnation is disclosure that the world is part of God's story. The task is not, then, how we can get God into the picture. It is rather how we understand our picture in terms of God's greater picture. I very much want to learn from spectacle, but the job is not to get God's story in spectacle, but to redefine spectacle in terms of God's story.

Second, this means that God's story is fleshy and engaged with human practices. The church that fails to take these things with the utmost seriousness is not Incarnational. To be fleshy and to pitch tent is to take seriously the enfleshed character of human life and the indigenous practices of that life. For this reason the church will take seriously the fleshy uses of image, sound as beat, and visualization. It will pitch tent with practices of convergence, bonding, and commitment. The Word will take on embodiment in spectacle, performance, soul music, and dance.

Again, the church has practices: the practices of worship, prayer, thanksgiving, evangelical and prophetic witness, hospitality—especially to the poor, peaceableness, justice, compassion, and service among others. These are crucial to the work of a faithful church.

I will not be discussing the desperately important roles of small-group life or that of discipling, or the crucial role of people finding their ministry. None of these can be excerpted from the life of a faithful church, but they are more than we can handle in the space here. My focus is on worship as Word and what it means for worship to be fleshy and to pitch tent with the people of an electronic culture.

Worship is the celebration and dramatization of God's story. It is the glorification of God as the Gracious Creator, Redeemer, and Ongoing Presence in that story. It is a story of the goodness of creation, of its defilement in sin, of its redemption through Christ, of a community called out to enact and embody that story, of the struggle of faithfulness in history and life, and it is a story that awaits an ultimate reign and seeks an intrinsic faithfulness to that reign where all will be one and will live with God forever. It is the act of making holy everything that is of the creation.[3] It is calling people to acknowledge who they are as God's creation and Whose they are.

To be faithful to this story, three things will characterize my approach. First, it will be formed in its themes by the lectionary. The lectionary is the best tool we have to deal with Scripture in its wholeness. The lectionary was created to encourage public reading of Scripture, and not necessarily as a sermon-planning regimen. Many clergy today design worship and preach from too small a portion of Scripture, usually the ones that appeal most to them. We need a broader exposure to the sweep of Scripture. Those who avoid or truncate Scripture for the sake of the moment, make a fundamental mistake for the sake of "relevance."

Second, the structure of worship visualized here will be governed by its traditional pattern. That is, it will be organized in terms of a fourfold structure of Entrance or Gathering, Proclamation and Response, Thanksgiving and Communion, and Sending Forth. Such a structure provides the flexibility required for different situations, but it also expresses the biblical, historical, and theological integrity of Christian worship.[4]

Third, I am a Wesleyan and I can no more avoid my own denominational tradition than I can breathe. My approach will therefore be Methodist, not because I want to claim a supremacy for that tradition, but because a church cannot be a tradition in general. When a congregation is under such pretense in the United States, it is usually in service to a consumerist tradition and engaged in the service of a false deity. At the same time, the tradition of the church is a lot like the Sante Fe Trail, as it runs from Kansas City to Sante Fe, New Mexico. I remember that when I came to Kansas City, I had an image in my mind of a couple of wagon ruts heading southwest across the prairie. I learned shortly after my arrival that sometimes the trail was several miles wide. So it is with the tradition of the church. I cannot be on all those trails at one time.

Further, I want to design worship for an electronic culture that is fleshy and pitches tent with the indigenous practices of that culture. In terms of what follows I want to design worship that has as a basic characteristic "the construction of an experience."[5] Worship will learn from spectacle. It will make use of the pacing, rhythm, and participation of performance. It will work with the soul music of the people gathered. And it will engage people in movement and dance. It will take convergence and the practice of meaning in experience with the utmost seriousness. And, finally, it will use electronic "critique" to offer worship that is alternative, oppositional, and subversive to the dominant order.

All this is obviously a tall order—especially for one who is admittedly not designing multiple worship services each week. What follows here will inevitably take on a kind of "engineered" effect. I regret this, but my interest is to illustrate that it can be done, to bear witness to the fact that I have seen it done. I apologize ahead of time that it may be a bit too contrived because I am combining elements that show up in part in many congregations. For example, I am going to use a significant amount of popular music throughout the chapter. Most churches will not use popular music on this scale. I do so because I want to demonstrate how it can be appropriated.

I also remember that worship is an art. Durkheim says somewhere that there is no fully reflective art, meaning, I take it, that art always outruns the thinking and the discourse about it. This is certainly true in what follows. My task is to put before us an integration of what has gone before. It certainly will not be enough for the sensitive pastor and layperson who put together a worship service that glorifies God and brings people to the healing of soul on a week-by-week basis at a fixed time and location. Still, I do believe that it does offer a faithful direction for people who engage the world in images, beat, and visualization.[6]

Worship As Experience

Let me suggest then an approach to worship that attempts to demonstrate the practices developed above and their place in a worship design. The theme for the service will be Incarnation and will use lections from that Sunday in the church year. The Scriptures on that day are: John 1:1–18; Heb. 1:1–4; Isa. 52:7–10; and Ps. 98. The message title is "The God Who Pitches Tent."

The format for doing so is threefold: First, I need to set the stage for the leadership team. Second, we need to describe the range of factors at work simultaneously in the service. Third, we need to give attention to the dynamics of flow used in the service. Do I need to say, again, that this is not the only way to do it? It is one way to encourage a plethora of designs.

Setting the Stage

First, I envision a band using contemporary instrumentation such as keyboard, guitars, bass, drums, and other available instruments that make a good "mix." Second, the band is to be joined by four to six singers—each with a microphone—who can provide good volume for not only their own singing but in leading the congregation and in giving full sound to the gathering. It will be helpful also to "mike" the congregation, provided sufficient technology is available so that a fuller voiced singing can be encouraged. This will require coordination of their vocal participation with the music and voices of the leadership team, but this can be done if such technology is available. I see an area up front that is cleared of pulpit and other furniture, except what is necessary for the enactment of the liturgy. The room needs to be one that can be filled to at least 80 percent occupancy. This figure may not be possible at first, but it is one that is reasonable to foresee. The point is that the room should not be too large. Don't get thirty people lost in an auditorium built for several hundred.

The Range of Factors

In this setting careful attention is given to image, beat, visualization, spectacle, performance, soul music, dance, convergence, meaning in experience, bonding, and commitment. It will also develop electronic critique and offer alternative, oppositional, and subversive experience to the dominant order. All of these are to be offered to the glory of God and to the goodness and holiness of God's creation and creatures, to God's story and our story within it as this is revealed in God's Word taking on human flesh and indigenous practices.

A few suggestions make this more concrete. I see a room with colorful banners that bespeak God's story. Some churches have the technology to project these "banners" on the wall. Six or eight of these around the walls of the room could very well address the stories of creation, sin, Incarnation, Atonement, Resurrection, the mission of the church, the Reign of God. Other themes could be those of Servanthood, Justice, Peace, Evangelism, Love, Faith, Hope, and so on. These banners shall reflect these themes in word and image. The room needs at least one large screen, preferably two or more. Overhead projectors can be used, but much more sophisticated technology is available, including TV monitors, LCD projectors, and so forth. Special lighting can be developed that can be used in connection with the band so that it pulses with their beat. It can also be used to slow pace and to focus on key persons and moments in the service.

The lighting should reflect the liturgical colors of the time of the church year. This can be done simply by using two grids of light. One grid will be at the very back of the worship center and reflect on that wall. Here a variety of colors can be used, especially those appropriate to the church year. At the front of this worship center can be another grid that is made up primarily of white light that can give sufficient illumination to the full staging area. This forward grid can be used for spotlights and for moving lights that sweep the congregation at times when full overt participation is indicated. Using grids like these provides color lighting and illumination that can be directed to a focus, but which do not create glare making it impossible to see the screens used for projections.[7]

A good collection of soul music from a genre that speaks to this congregation needs to be researched and thought through in terms of the theme of Incarnation, songs appropriate to each structural aspect of the worship service. Some of these songs need to represent messages from the dominant culture. In response to these, other songs need to be found that stand in opposition to them, as I will demonstrate below. Short dramas can be developed for different aspects of the service.

These should not be used every Sunday, but made available on a continual basis. Forms of electronic critique need to be developed for use in the service at critical points where a prophetic word is spoken.

Many possible visual resources can be used here. Photographs taken during the previous week capturing moments in the congregation's life together can be displayed: pictures of a church outing, a mission program, a funeral, a baptism, a Sunday school class, the church staff, work on a Habitat for Humanity house. Children's art from the Sunday school is a wonderful source of visuals. This work can anticipate the theme of a worship service. These also become a part of the church's growing file of resources. News headlines, pictures from the daily newspapers, comments from the news, phrases from the lectionary, cartoons, and a host of images now available on computer programs—all offer an array of possibilities.

The Dynamics of Flow

Attention to the construction of the liturgy as an experience requires focus on the basic integrity of Christian worship (gathering, proclamation and response, thanksgiving, sending forth) and on spectacle and the practice of performance with its characteristics of pacing, rhythm, and participation. I see, for example, a time of extended invocation of the Spirit that begins before the appointed hour in which a "warm up" occurs. This involves the band and singers offering a ten-minute time of singing and prayer. The prayer can be done in a solo or group song, or it can be spoken, usually as a voice-over with background music. It can, of course, be both.

Participation of the gathering congregation will be encouraged either through singing with the leadership team, or by clapping and standing while doing movements with appropriate gestures, or both. These songs can be selected with the theme of Incarnation and brief, key phrases from the lections can be projected on one screen as the songs are sung from yet another. The point is to create a sense of expectancy and readiness about the morning and the themes of faithful life to be addressed. This work (liturgy) will be continued throughout the remainder of the structure, giving attention to the character of performance. Below I will illustrate this in more concrete detail.

111

Several additional considerations relate importantly to the flow. Stop and start moments need to be eliminated. The service will be designed to flow from one point to the next without such "instructions" as "Now we are going to pray" or "Now we are going to sing." These can be clearly indicated without such intrusion into the experience. Moreover, music will be virtually continuous throughout the service, though silence can be very important. Prayers, litanies, and responses can be done as voice-overs and they can be sung. The flow of the mood of the service can be suggested by the movement of the music, especially in transitions.

Clearly, the overall course of the service is in terms of these dynamics. The Eucharist during the time of the thanksgiving will be the celebrative climax of the service. As such, the design of the worship will move toward this phase as a heightened sense of the Real Presence of Christ. The dynamic here is one that begins in the gravity of Christ's betrayal, torture, and crucifixion, which moves to a proclamation of his resurrection and of the vision of his great banquet in the reign of God. The Eucharist is the time to revel in the welcome table, to experience the presence of Christ, and to celebrate life together. It is out of this context that the congregation is sent forth to be God's people in the world.

To put it in a word or a visual, the worship suggests something like a moving gestalt, a fully orbed dynamic of soul music, embodied movement, pervasive visualization, with spoken words coming at the right time in an environmentally cohesive surrounding. It is a gestalt constructed in experience that attempts to bear the story of God, to celebrate that story, to glorify God, and to counter the false gods of a dominant order. It is a Scripture-infused, liturgically structured event that enfleshes itself with the people gathered and pitches tent with their basic practices of sensing, feeling, thinking, knowing, meaning, and identity. It is an event that empowers people to be disciples and to move into mission in a world that God clearly loves.[8]

CHAPTER ELEVEN

An Illustrated Worship Service

To illustrate the previous chapter, let us work with several genres of music and describe a worship service using these genres at four moments in the service. Space limitations prevent going into more detail. The four times to discuss are those of invocation (warm up), confession and pardon, Scripture and message, and Eucharist. These four movements in worship are performed with country music, popular music, rock, and rap.[1] I do not understand these as necessarily the most important genres, but simply as diverse and offering useful ways to tease out the implications of the spectacle of worship.

Further, I am not suggesting that this diversity of music be used in one service, but rather I am drawing from different genres simply to demonstrate possible uses. Finally, I am not using contemporary praise music because it is widely used and some of it is good, but I want to work with secular music instead.[2]

Gathering (Warm Up) with Country Music

In the gathering the band begins with a fast-paced version of "Will the Circle Be Unbroken?" The words are displayed on the screen to allow the congregation to sing with the leadership team. Lights flash across the congregation in a layered way. That is, different colors of light sweep across different rows of seats. Hangings in the room suggest the colors of the church year and one screen indicates what these are and what they symbolize. The lighting on the back grid uses these colors. The bulletin can also be used to describe briefly the meaning of the colors and other key symbolization in the service, so that worshipers can take this with them as they leave. The songs are primarily done to a syncopated beat, and the congregation engages in clapping along with the music. The tempo of the movement of the lights increases during the singing of the chorus, encouraging the congregation to join in more fully. A dance group moves into the aisles during the singing of the song, encouraging the congregation to move with them. Selections from Ps. 98 and from Isa. 52 are flashed on the different screens throughout the gathering time.

With the end of the first song the music modulates toward the next phase and the mood and the pace of the music change. The song is "Just a Closer Walk with Thee." It is done slowly and in a more pensive mood, but in syncopated beat. It may use a soloist. The lights focus steadily either on the soloist and the one offering the prayer or on the Cross or other worship center. The song takes on a prayerlike quality. Upon the completion of two verses and choruses the music moves into the background and a voice-over begins a prayer calling upon the Holy Spirit and giving thanks for God's presence with us. It presages the incarnational theme of the day. With the ending of the prayer the music modulates again into an upbeat, faster pace with the song "I Saw the Light." Here the congregation will be encouraged to stand and clap with the music. Words are displayed on one screen along with other visuals on the others. Visuals here may be used to capture special events of the previous week in the church or community so as to bring these to the time of celebration of God's presence.[3]

Confession and Pardon: Popular Music

Some of those working on contemporary worship argue that confession of sin should not be used during seeker services that expose the Christian way for the first time to uninformed visitors or guests. Others more carefully observe that the issue is not whether there is a confession of sin or not, but rather how it is done. Stanley Hauerwas is correct when he says that one cannot be a Christian without learning that one is a sinner.[4] The issue is: Does it address people in indigenous forms? Does it speak to the heart? Because people find the most convincing narratives of their lives in popular music, it offers significant approaches to both confession and pardon. I hope it is clear that I am not approaching this music in terms of what it says in itself—whatever in the world that may mean—but rather from a perspective that "reads/sees/views/hears" it in terms of Christian faith.

114

By using popular music, confession can be an opportunity to do both a critique of the dominant culture as corporate sin and to move toward pardon and an alternative. I think here of Frank Sinatra's rendition of "My Way." It is a very popular song and I know of no other that better exemplifies wanting to live life on one's own terms. It is a classic case of the glorification of self-sufficiency, a denial of God's story. I can visualize a spirited singing of the song throughout the first verse or so with visuals of Frank or other illustrations of it, such as headlines or comments or poems like "I am the master of my fate, the captain of my soul."[5] Or perhaps one could use some quote from John Wayne that especially champions self-sufficiency.[6]

Imagine then moving the song perhaps into a minor key, or at least into the background, and a visual that quotes a news article that says: "Sources close to the Frank Sinatra family report that before his death Sinatra suffered from Alzheimer's disease the last years of his life. Sinatra, one of the most popular singers in America for more there fifty years is best known for his rendition of 'My Way.' " This can be read by a voice in a neutral journalistic fashion. It is not my intent to insult Sinatra here. His story of doing things "my way" is our story too.

Then another voice moves into a prayer of forgiveness confessing that we *all* seem to want to live life our way, that we want to live life on our own terms. The prayer calls us to a more realistic assessment of the limitations of life and of our need for others and especially for the sustenance and guidance of God.

The move to pardon can use a song like "People" ("People who need people are the luckiest people in the world").[7] The pardon can be given while the tune only is played or while the song is sung quietly in the background. Here a hymn can be also be used. "Great Is Thy Faithfulness" is a prayer unto itself and can be used instead of a voice-over. During the pardon the lection from Hebrews can be displayed on-screen or it can be incorporated into the prayer of forgiveness, or both.

Another popular music variation on this is the song "I'm Always Chasing Rainbows" where we find the line "all my schemes are just like all my dreams ending in the sky." This nuances the confession differently since it owns up to the fact that one's schemes and dreams evaporate and do not take on any kind of reality, but it does address the widespread desire to live life on one's own terms. In the pardon a popular song like "Somewhere," which proclaims that there is "a place for us, a time and place for us" offers hope.[8] Here the proclamation of forgiveness in a voice-over can base this hope in what God has done for us. As William B. McClain once said to me: We worship the God who gets with us in order to get to us.

Because popular music provides the narratives of so many people's lives, I want them in the liturgy and placed in the framework of the larger story of God's work in Christ. This placement involves not only an appreciation for certain forms of yearning and narrative display in popular music, but also calls into question claims from this music that will not stand the scrutiny of a prophetic faith. DC Talk has excellent "confessions" in its album *Jesus Freak* where some half dozen songs are excellent confessions in rock and rap formats.[9]

I do not, however, see this as a time of moralizing about the faith. That is, we do not need prayers that say things like: "We thank you, God, for freeing us from these worldly ways of seeing things." Rather, these prayers of confession name the fact that we do, indeed, seek to live our lives in these terms and that our only hope is the transformative power of God's grace working in the concrete practices of our everyday lives. We also don't need a bunch of "if . . . then prayers": "If we would just stop doing these things, our lives would be better." That's the problem, either we will not, we cannot, or we cannot will to do otherwise.[10] This is what the bondage of sin is about! The last thing we need is clergy and laity doing "if only" complaints. "If only" lamentation is the last, desperate move of those who have run out of sound theology.

The further concern is the formation of how we as the people of God converge popular music. Worship that engages the popular culture and places it within the Christian story offers new forms of convergence that call into question the offerings of the dominant culture and provide new ways of appropriating them. Further, worship "constructs" different structures from the senses, feelings, thinking, knowing, commitment, and bonding. The purpose of worship is not merely about changing people's *views*, it's about glorification of the God who changes our very natures.

Scripture and Sermon: Rock Music and Story

The central text for the sermon is "the Word became flesh and dwelt with us." The song "What if God Were One of Us?" sung by Joan Osborne, is very appropriate for use with the Scripture reading.[11] It raises the question in a rock format in a way that "works" in this context. One of the lyrics, for example, asks What if God were "a stranger on the bus trying to make his way home." For those who listen to rock, it will engage them in the theme of the service. I see the beginning of the Scripture reading time as one when the song is played. As it moves into the background, the Scripture can be read by a man and a woman together in a "duet" fashion, suggesting the full humanity of God in Christ.[12]

The sermon, or message, is ten minutes long with time for a brief treatment of the text in terms of its centrality in the church's understanding of God pitching tent with us in Christ. Most of the sermon, about six minutes, will be given over to a story. This story will use the dynamic Simon Frith identifies as description, feeling, and identity.

I'd like to tell William K. McElvaney's story here. When Bill was president of Saint Paul School of Theology, he had to pick up a visiting dignitary and lecturer at the Kansas City International Airport, which is about twenty miles north of the city. To get there you have to cross the Paseo Bridge, a four-lane crossing, high above the Missouri River. As he reached a point about a half mile from the bridge, the traffic completely stopped. Nothing moved. He was there for some time and worried about getting to the airport on time. After about fifteen minutes, the traffic started up and moved quickly over the bridge. Bill looked for signs of a collision, broken glass, sheared metal, anything to explain the delay. He saw nothing.

The next morning he was curious to find out what happened so he checked the newspaper. In it he found out that a man, quite despondent, stopped his car in the outside lane of the bridge, got out, crawled over the rail, and climbed down into the support structure of the bridge waiting to get the final desperation to jump to his death. People who saw this called the police and a patrol wagon came. The officers spoke to him from the top of the bridge trying to get him to come up and talk, which he refused. Meanwhile, another patrolman put on a harness with a long rope attached. The other end was tied to the patrol wagon and the officer went over the side of the bridge, climbing down slowly to reach the man. As the officer moved toward him he spoke softly and assured the man that things could get better and that the people there wanted to help him. From the top of the bridge the other police continued to feed him rope so that he could move closer. The slack, however, increased because of the route he had to take.

Moving carefully toward him, the patrolman finally got within arm's reach of the despondent man. As he did, the man jumped. But the patrolman, timing his own leap with the man's, caught him in mid-air, wrapping both arms and both legs around him in tight embrace. They then fell together until the slack in the rope ran out a good many feet below. They bounced at the end of the rope, swinging back and forth over that yawning river.

Up on the bridge the police heard the patrolman yelling at the top of his lungs: "If you go, I go! Because I'm going to hold on to you until hell freezes over!"

The message, the narrative, ends with the comment: "I don't know what kind of hell you're caught up in this morning, but I want you to know that we worship a God who refuses to leave us. We are not only in God's hands but wrapped about by divine 'arms and legs' in an embrace that will not let us go until hell freezes over. This is the assurance of the God who becomes human in Christ."

I see this story beginning in a description of a man in obvious desperation. The narrative of the heroic efforts of the police build the poignancy of the occasion. When the policeman leaps with him and catches him in the open air, falling with him and yelling out his intention to stay with him, the listener's feelings reach an apex. When the sermon then takes the turn of the kind of "hell" or desperation people in the congregation face on that day, it raises the question of identity. It descriptively invokes the desperation of those present, it provides vivid emotive engagement and raises sharply the identity question in terms of one's own life.

The congregation is then invited to talk with a neighbor about his or her reflections on God's becoming human in Christ and pitching tent with us. The congregation is given about five minutes to talk among themselves while a reprise of "What if God Were One of Us?" is played as background music. At this point the visuals are still, but pick up the themes of Christ pitching tent with us. The pastor then asks if anyone would like to share a thought with the congregation. Three or four of these can then be briefly shared. As this ends, the music begins a transition into the Eucharist.

Eucharist, Drama, and Andrew Lloyd Webber

In the Eucharist I see here the use of a dramatization in place of the reading of the Great Thanksgiving. I saw this as it was done by a group of Russian youth at the North Alabama International Peace Camp at Lake Sumatonga under the direction of Nina Reeves, the long-time and charismatic leader of youth in the United Methodist Church there.

Six youth were positioned on the stage, each with a different but very difficult condition: one with deep depression contemplating suicide, one with a severe crippling, one abjectly alone, one hungry, and one poor. Another youth was the Christ who came to the aid of each one and healed the person. Each time this happened, however, Christ took on the condition of that person and, after doing so, was crucified by those who had been "healed." The scene then went completely dark until striking light appeared in the center of the stage and the Resurrection occurred.

In addition to the dramatization, I would like the song "Pie Jesu" with music by Andrew Lloyd Webber used. Done as a soprano solo it speaks to the drama and to the Eucharist with the words in translation from the Latin: "Merciful Jesus, who takest away the sins of the world, grant them peace. O Lamb of God who takest away the sins of the world, grant them eternal rest." This English translation would be displayed on-screen as the drama unfolded.[13]

With the coming of total darkness the music stops and the congregation sits in silence for a full minute or two. After what will seem like a long time, I visualize a light that begins to shine from a point slightly above where Christ was crucified.

This light has a very small aperture but can cast a beam across the room. With this light a soprano sings, at first quietly and without accompaniment, "Prepare ye the way of the Lord." As she sings, the light expands its sweep and magnitude and the volume of the song increases. Instruments join in on the third verse and the congregation is cued in to sing also as the words appear on the screen. The volume of the song continues to increase with the growing volume of light in

119

the sanctuary. In a room full of sound and light the elements are then received in this celebration of the Resurrection.

There need to be enough stations for the distribution of the bread and wine so that the entire congregation can be served in five minutes. As they are served the elements, key phrases of the Great Thanksgiving flash on the other screen, interpersed with images of the Eucharist. The Eucharist ends with prayer as the music continues in the background.

These four aspects of the liturgy illustrate that the ingredients of spectacle can be used within the basic traditional structure of worship using the lectionary.

Liturgy As the Work of a Team

It is clear that worship of this kind cannot be done by one person. Moreover, the late Saturday night planning for Sunday morning will not do. It will require a team doing ongoing work. Some will be involved in research on appropriate soul music, while others will be engaged in finding or developing images and videos. Some will be working on issues of flow and the construction of the experience of worship; others will be searching for, developing, and rehearsing mini-dramas and brief skits. Musicians will be developing new music and working with liturgists to integrate and coordinate their presentations. I also see, for example, the benefit of having several teams working on materials with each responsible for a different Sunday. Several teams of youth can take video cameras to mission points and develop three-minute videos on these for presentation to the congregation. Many of these youth already have the skill to do this.[14]

It is also clear that we do not know how to do many of the things outlined here, for example, congregational movement, dance, and appropriate gestures. We need a range of experimental settings where things can be developed and tried out without failure being as disastrous as it could be during a regular service. Church camps and youth and young adult events are already experimenting with such, and many of them are doing very good work. This needs to be encouraged and taken back to the home churches. People in small groups can be encouraged to try out new worship formats and to become adept at these practices.

What about the small church? A small church should not attempt to change the present service of worship but should instead add another service. The timing may not be right, however, to do this immediately. Instead, a Bible study or prayer group should be formed that will use electronic practices as part of their meetings. Such settings can develop dance as part of their time together. As these grow in size, they can be occasions for developing worship appropriate to those gathered. The development of images, music, and light may be smaller in scale, but higher participation by those in the group can offset these kinds of disadvantages. A small group can do these things and make up in the intensity of the group's relationships and intimacy what may be lacking in the complexity and magnitude of a large gathering. Certainly the use of video, soul music, creative imagery, and dance are not excluded by the factor of size. In fact, much of the movement and dance will require small group efforts before they can be appropriated by the larger congregation.

The point is that a group's creativity and ingenuity can address these kinds of questions and that we need these things emerging from the grass roots. Church size is not prohibitive.

Convergence Without End

The coming and convergence of electronic culture is a momentous time. It is one of the major challenges facing the church and the wider society. It is not an unalloyed good. It is not an unmitigated evil. It brings with it indigenous practices, as I have tried to demonstrate. Emergent forms of thinking and knowing are already surfacing. The reconstruction of human beings in their sensing, feelings, and experience of the body is already underway. New ways to approach the world have been in operation for some time. The religious lives of generations raised under the influence of electronic culture have already changed.

Much of electronic culture is based in a consumerist story that has crept into a host of the forms of life at work in the wider society and in the church. This is a profoundly distorted story. It will require alternative, oppositional, and subversive resistance.

But such resistance cannot be simply based in a negative of opposition. The resistance will need a story of its own, one more powerful than the consumerist. This story will be one that gives an ultimate significance to human beings, to social and historical life, a story adequate to the haunting reality of death that cannot be overcome by technology. It will be a story that addresses the human limits and failure that dog every step of electronic "progress." It will be a story adequate to the longings and yearnings of human beings, one not lost finally in despair or in the self-deception of arrogance. The story will be one that combines the vision of justice, peace, and genuine freedom. Electronic culture has enormous capacities for inequality, for sanitized violence, and for the reduction of freedom to "personal choice." Any story that does not address these matters is an ideological fiction designed to serve the interests of the principalities and powers.

As human beings, we cannot avoid commitment to a basic trust, one that lies beyond our proof and beyond our capacity to eradicate it. Even nihilism is an unproven confidence in the vacuity of life. I place my trust in the Christian story, the story of the God who becomes human, who becomes embodied and takes up residence with us in the practices of ordinary life. I do not doubt that this God will raise up people to meet the challenges before us in the world now taking form. The question is really whether those in the churches today will be part of that venture.

The call here is for a church that will "imitate" Christ to pitch tent, to embody itself, to take form in the indigenous practices of our time, not for the purpose of accommodation to the world but rather to be God's people. It is a twofold effort: To join the practices of an electronic culture, on the one hand, and to keep faith with the story of Christ, on the other. In worship this will mean taking up the practices of spectacle and faithfulness to the biblical narrative and to the integrity of Christian liturgy.

Chapter One

1. Walter Ong, *The Presence of the Word* (Minneapolis: University of Minnesota Press, 1967), 6, 190.

2. Constance Classen, David Howes, and Anthony Synnott, *Aroma: The Cultural History of Smell* (New York: Routledge, 1994). See also Constance Classen, *Worlds of Sense: Exploring the Senses in History and Across Cultures* (New York: Routledge, 1993).

3. *Presence of the Word,* 3–7.

4. See, for example, the magazine *Wired* and note its radically different format, its language, and its framing of questions and issues.

5. Marshall McLuhan, *Understanding Media* (New York: The New American Library, 1964), 35.

6. Ibid., 23; see ix, 23, 24, 35.

7. Ibid., 19.

8. Ibid., 27.

9. Matt Wray and Annalee Newitz, eds., *White Trash: Race and Class in America* (New York: Routledge, 1997).

10. I am indebted here to Alasdair MacIntyre, *After Virtue: A Study in Moral Theory,* 2nd ed. (Notre Dame, Ind.: Notre Dame University Press, 1984), *passim,* which informs my treatment here.

Chapter Two

1. Jean Baudrillard, *Simulations,* trans. Paul Foss, Paul Patton, Philip Beitchman (New York: Semiotext(e), Inc., 1983), 11.

2. Neil Postman, *Amusing Ourselves to Death* (New York: Penguin, 1985).

3. Ibid., 24.

4. See Robert Fowler, "How the Secondary Orality of the Electronic Age Can Awaken Us to the Primary Orality of Antiquity or What Hypertext Can Teach Us About the Bible with Reflections on the Ethical and Political Issues of the Electronic Frontier" (paper presented at the Semiotics and Exegesis Section SBL Annual Meeting, Chicago, Ill., Nov. 19, 1994).

5. Marius Von Senden, *Space and Sight* (New York: The Free Press, 1960), quoted in S. Morris Engel, *The Study of Philosophy,* 2nd ed. (San Diego: Collegiate Press, 1987), 265–67.

6. Ron Burnett, *Cultures of Vision* (Bloomington: University of Indiana Press, 1995), 237.

7. I am indebted to a conversation with Larry Hollon for this observation.

8. Janice Radway, *Reading the Romance: Women, Patriarchy, and Popular Literature* (London: Verso, 1987); Ien Ang, *Watching Dallas: Soap Opera and the Melodramatic Imagination* (London: Metheun, 1985); and Tricia Rose, *Black Noise: Rap Music and Black Culture in Contemporary America* (Hanover, N.H.: Wesleyan University Press, 1994. See the developing literature in this area: James Scott, *Weapons of the Weak: Everyday Forms of Peasant Resistance* (New Haven, Conn.: Yale University Press, 1985); Mikhail Bakhtin, *Rabelais and His World*, trans. Helene Iswolsky (Bloomington: Indiana University Press, 1984); Eugene D. Genovese, *"Roll, Jordan, Roll": The World the Slaves Made* (New York: Vintage, 1974); Vaclav Havel, *Living in Truth: Twenty-two Essays Published on the Occasion of the Award of the Erasmus Prize to Vaclav Havel,* ed. Jan Vladislav (London: Faber & Faber, 1986). This literature demonstrates the capacity of ordinary people to resist an array of oppressive settings.

9. Susan Mitchell, "How to Talk to Young Adults," *American Demographics,* 15, 4 (April 1993), 53–54.

10. Clifford Geertz, *The Interpretation of Cultures* (New York: Basic, 1973).

11. Quoted in Howard A. Snyder, *EarthCurrents: The Struggle for the World's Soul* (Nashville: Abingdon, 1995), 109.

12. *No Sense of Place: The Impact of Electronic Media on Social Behavior* (New York: Oxford University Press, 1985), 326.

13. Wade Clark Roof, *A Generation of Seekers* (San Francisco: HarperSanFrancisco, 1993), 134.

14. Ibid., 135.

15. Ibid.

16. Ibid.

Chapter Three

1. *Generation of Seekers,* 54.

2. Chukwulozie Anyanwu, "Sound As Ultimate Reality and Meaning: The Mode of Knowing Reality in African Thought," *Ultimate Reality and Meaning* 10, 1 (March 1987).

3. Martin Jay, "Scopic Regimes of Modernity," in S. Lash and J. Friedman, eds. *Modernity and Identity* (Oxford: Blackwell, 1992).

4. Quoted in Chris Jenks, ed., *Visual Culture* (London: Routledge), 1995, 14.

5. Mickey Hart, *Drumming at the Edge of Magic* (San Francisco: HarperSanFrancisco, 1990), 119.

6. For a fine account of Hank Williams's life, see Roger M. Williams, *Sing a Sad Song: The Life of Hank Williams* (Chicago: University of Illinois Press, 1981).

7. See Peter Guralnick's fine treatment of these events in *Last Train to Memphis: The Rise of Elvis Presley* (New York: Little, Brown and Company, 1994), 84–87, 93–97.

8. Quoted in Ed Ward, Geoffrey Stokes, and Ken Tucker, *Rock of Ages: The Rolling Stone History of Rock & Roll* (New York: Rolling Stone, 1986), 293–94. I am indebted to Susan McClary for calling this to my attention in her fine article, "Same As It Ever Was: Youth Culture and Music," in *Microphone Fiends: Youth Music & Youth Culture,* ed. Andrew Ross and Tricia Rose (New York: Routledge, 1994), 34–35.

9. "Same As It Ever Was," *Microphone Fiends,* 36.

10. Ibid.

11. Winstead is pastor of North Springs United Methodist Church in Atlanta.

12. I am indebted to Hess B. "Doc" Hall Jr., a staff person at North Springs United Methodist Church in Atlanta, who pointed out this pattern of audience participation in Elvis's singing of "Jailhouse Rock."

13. Daniel Yankelovich, *New Rules: Searching for Self-Fulfillment in a World Turned Upside Down* (New York: Random House, 1981), 21.

14. I am indebted here to Quentin J. Schultze et al., *Dancing in the Dark: Youth, Popular Culture, and the Electronic Media* (Grand Rapids, Mich.: Eerdmans, 1991), 122–24.

Chapter Four

1. David Halberstam, *October 1964* (New York: Villard, 1994), 354–55.

2. Lawrence Grossberg, "Is Anybody Listening? Does Anybody Care? On Talking About the 'State of Rock,' " in *Microphone Fiends,* 41–42.

3. Ibid., 49.

4. Ibid., 54. Italics mine.

5. Ibid. Italics mine.

6. Jay Cocks, "Sing a Song of Seeing," *Time,* 26 December 1983, 54. Italics mine.

7. Nicolas Zill and John Robinson, "The Generation X Difference," *American Demographics* 17, 4 (April 1995), 24–29, 32–33.

8. Howard A. Snyder, *EarthCurrents: The Struggle for the World's Soul* (Nashville: Abingdon, 1995), 115.

9. Hanspeter Krellmann, *The New Grove Music Dictionary of Music and Musicians,* ed. Stanley Sadie (London: Macmillan, 1980), 13:707. I am indebted to Howard Johnson for calling the Krellman article to my attention.

Chapter Five

1. "Edelweiss," Williamson Music Co., 1959. Words and music by Richard Rodgers and Oscar Hammerstein II.

2. This is Randall Collins and Michael Makowsky's characterization of Durkheim's position. See their *Discovery of Society,* 5th ed. (New York: McGraw-Hill 1993), 105, 107. See also Emile Durkheim, *The Elementary Forms of Religious Life,* trans. Joseph Ward Swain (New York: Collier, 1961), and *The Division of Labor,* trans. George Simpson (New York: The Free Press, 1964).

3. Guy Debord, *The Society of the Spectacle* (Detroit: Black and Ted, 1976), 10.

4. Ibid., 12–13.

5. Karl Marx, *Capital: A Critique of Political Economy*, ed. Frederick Engels (New York: The Modern Library, 1906). See for example, 703–83.

6. Gerhard Lenski calls such societies horticultural. See his *Power and Privilege: A Theory of Stratification* (New York: McGraw-Hill, 1966), 117–41.

7. Yet, see Frederich Engel's letter to Joseph Bloch in Lewis S. Feuer, ed., *Marx & Engels: Basic Writings on Politics and Philosophy* (Garden City, N.Y.: Anchor, 1959), 397–400.

8. *Society of the Spectacle,* 180.

9. See John Eldridge and Lizzie Eldridge, *Raymond Williams: Making Connections* (New York: Routledge, 1994), 45–75. I am indebted to Stanley Hauerwas for calling this to my attention. See his "In Defense of Cultural Christianity: Reflections on Going to Church." Mimeo.

Chapter Six

1. Walter Ong, *The Presence of the Word* (Minneapolis: University of Minnesota, 1967), 115. See also 122, 123, 128.
2. John Chernoff, *African Rhythm and African Sensibility: Aesthetics and Social Action in African Musical Idioms* (Chicago: University of Chicago Press, 1979). Quoted in Mickey Hart, *Drumming at the Edge of Magic* (San Francisco: Harper, 1990), 197.
3. *Drumming at the Edge of Magic,* 197.
4. Tricia Rose, *Black Noise: Rap Music and Black Culture in Contemporary America* (Hanover, N.H.: Wesleyan University Press, 1994), 66.
5. Walter Ong, *Orality and Literacy* (London: Routledge, 1982), 71–74.
6. *Drumming at the Edge of Magic,* 18.
7. I have made the case for this in another context. *White Soul* (Nashville: Abingdon, 1997).
8. See Rose, *Black Noise.*
9. Ruth Finnegan, *The Hidden Musicians* (Cambridge: Cambridge University Press, 1989).
10. My point here is not to turn aesthetics judgments into extrinsic methods of doing ethics, since I suspect that would be self-defeating in that it would turn an intrinsic aesthetic expression (the aim of beauty) into a tool (a means) primarily. Rather, I would like to see the coincidence of intrinsic beauty and intrinsic good as able to grasp the commitment of people and to form their basic dispositions. Conversely, such an approach could display wrong as hideous and ghastly.
11. Doug Adams, *Congregational Dancing in Christian Worship* (San Francisco: The Sharing Company, 1971); Judith Lynne Hanna, *Dance, Sex and Gender* (Chicago: University of Chicago Press, 1988); and Sally Banes, *Writing Dancing in the Age of Postmodernism* (Hanover, N.H.: Wesleyan University Press, 1994), 333–40. The work by Banes is especially helpful in its attention to multicultural forms of dance and in its chapter on spectacle in the U.S. in the 1980s and 1990s.

Chapter Seven

1. Linda Kelly, *Deadheads: Behind the Scenes with the Family, Friends, and Followers of the Grateful Dead* (New York: Citadel, 1995).
2. Mark Johns, "The Rhetoric of Secondary Orality in Christian Homiletics: The Effects of the Electronic Media on Preaching" (master's thesis, University of Northern Iowa, December 1995), 36.
3. *Dancing in the Dark,* 149. Italics mine.
4. "Thick description" is clearly the language of Clifford Geertz in his *Interpretation of Cultures* (New York: Basic, 1973).
5. For evidence that this interest in "rush" is not simply an idiosyncrasy of our son, see Rebecca Piirto Heath, "You Can Buy a Thrill: Chasing the Ultimate Rush," *American Demographics,* 19, 6 (June 1997), 47–51.
6. Ibid., 49.
7. Ibid., 50.
8. Jennifer Gabriel, "Crazy for Sports," *The Kansas City Star,* 7 August 1997, E-1, E-2.
9. Simon Frith, *Performing Rites: On the Value of Popular Music* (Cambridge, Mass.: Harvard University Press 1996, 275.
10. Ibid.
11. I am using a formulation of John Miller Chernoff in his description of African drumming in Ghana. See *African Drumming and African Sensibility* (Chi-

cago: University of Chicago Press, 1979), 36, quoted in Frith, *Performing Rites,* 272.

12. "Is Anybody Listening? Does Anybody Care? On Talking About 'The State of Rock,' " in *Microphone Fiends,* 49.

Chapter Eight

1. See James Brook and Iain A. Boal, eds., *Resisting the Virtual Life: The Culture and Politics of Information* (San Francisco: City Lights, 1995), and Gail Dines and Jean M. Humez, eds., *Gender, Race and Class in Media: A Text-Reader* (Thousand Oaks, Calif.: Sage Publications, 1995).

2. I am indebted here to Stanley Hauerwas, *The Peaceable Kingdom: A Primer in Christian Ethics* (Notre Dame, Ind.: Notre Dame University Press, 1983), 28–29.

3. *A Generation of Seekers,* 200–203.

4. See here the work of Dean R. Hoge, Benton Johnson, and Donald A. Luidens, *Vanishing Boundaries: The Religion of Mainline Protestant Baby Boomers* (Louisville: Westminster/John Knox, 1994), 112–15, 138–43, 184–86.

5. Rom. 12:1–2.

6. 1 Cor. 9:22.

7. For example, Alasdair MacIntyre argues that reason is tradition-dependent in *Whose Justice—Whose Rationality* (Notre Dame, Ind.: Notre Dame University Press, 1988), 354–69. Richard Rorty maintains that the notion of "foundations of knowledge" takes its lead from the employment of "visual epistemological metaphors." See *Philosophy and the Mirror of Nature* (Princeton: Princeton University Press, 1979), 159. Michel Foucault claims that the text, discourse, and truth serve power in *Power/Knowledge: Selected Interviews & Other Writings, 1972–1977,* ed. Colin Gordon (New York: Pantheon, 1980), 109–33. Edward W. Said contends that Western discourse on "the Orient" is a body of power-knowledge relations. It is a European invention created to serve Western power and interests. In this connection, Said argues that in examining a text or discourse it is more important to know who says something and where and when it is said than what is said. See *Orientalism* (Harmondsworth, England: Penguin, 1985), 1–3. See also Said's *The World, the Text, and the Critic* (Cambridge, Mass.: Harvard University Press, 1983). Anthony Giddens observes the very ways we argue "are presumed in the use of language." See Giddens's "Reason Without Revolution? Habermas's *Theorie des kommunikativen Handelns*" in *Habermas and Modernity,* ed. Richard J. Bernstein, (Cambridge, Mass.: The MIT Press, 1985), 115. Jacques Derrida, in *Of Grammatology* (Baltimore: Johns Hopkins University Press, 1976), contends that the use of words depends not only on differentiation by the use of complex fields of polarities, but continually defers "meaning" throughout the entire system of language so that there is no "presence" of meaning in it.

Chapter Nine

1. Larry Hollon also reminds me of the self-immolation of the monk in Vietnam and the execution of a Vietcong soldier by a South Vietnamese soldier with a pistol at the moment the bullet is fired.

2. *Performing Rites,* 271. Italics mine.

3. Ibid.

4. Ibid.

5. The lyrics cited from "American Trilogy" reflect the version as Elvis performed it. The published version is copyrighted by Lewis Music Publishing Co., Inc., 1973.

6. Stanley Hauerwas makes this point throughout his writing.

Chapter Ten

1. See also Heb. 2:17.

2. See Constance Classen, *Worlds of Sense,* and Alasdair MacIntyre, *Whose Justice?*

3. See Don Saliers's definition of corporate worship as "the glorification of God and the sanctification of all that is creaturely" in "Our Liturgical Dilemma," *Circuit Rider* (December 94-January 95), 6. Saliers's treatment here offers a sensitive critique of contemporary worship and deserves prayerful consideration.

4. Indebtedness here goes to *The United Methodist Hymnal* (Nashville: The United Methodist Publishing House, 1989), 2.

5. Indebtedness in use of this language goes to Bill Easum, from an oral presentation at Platte Woods United Methodist Church in Platte Woods, Missouri, June 12, 1997.

6. Susan J. White addresses worship in relation to technological change. She deals with a different range of issues from those I work with here, but her work certainly deserves a careful reading. See her *Christian Worship and Technological Change* (Nashville: Abingdon, 1994).

7. I am indebted here to Marsha Morgan who suggested this after being at a national youth meeting of the Reorganized Church of Jesus Christ of Latter-Day Saints.

8. In planning worship, Word Music provides a resource, *Songs for Praise and Worship/Worship Planner Edition* (888–324–9673); a careful and detailed planning guide is *Come Celebrate: A Guide for Planning Contemporary Worship* by Cathy Townley and Mike Graham (Nashville: Abingdon, 1995). It also has a CD and songbook.

Chapter Eleven

1. It should be clear that licensing is required for the use of all copyrighted songs.

2. Some sources for contemporary Christian music are: Hosanna Integrity Music (800–877–4443); Maranatha! Music (800–444–4012); Saddleback Praises (800–458–2772); Interlinc provides each quarter CDs and tapes of Christian music, P.O. Box 680848, Franklin, TN 37068. I especially like the work of Jim and Jean Strathdee, Caliche Records, P.O. Box 1735, Ridgecrest, CA 93555; Larry Olson and Dakota Road Music (605–331–4420), P.O. Box 90344, Sioux Falls, SD 57109; Wellsprings Unlimited, 12424 Orchard Road, Minnetonka, MN 55305; and Dust and Ashes (615–292–3725), 2905 Snowden Road, Nashville, TN 37204. One does need licensing to use this music. Christian Copyright Licensing, Inc., 6130 N.E. 78th, Suite C-11, Portland, OR 97218 provides copyright privileges for a great many songs and their charge is based on the size of the congregation.

3. A good resource for country music, organized according to themes, is Dorothy Horstman, *Sing Your Heart Out, Country Boy* (Nashville: Vanderbilt University Press, 1995). It does not, however, feature more recent music.

4. Stanley Hauerwas, *After Christendom: How the Church Is to Behave if Freedom, Justice, and a Christian Nation Are Bad Ideas* (Nashville: Abingdon, 1991), 108–9.

5. John Bartlett, *Familiar Quotations* (Toronto: Little, Brown and Company, 1968) a poem by William Ernest Henley, *Echoes IV, In Memoriam R. T. Hamilton Bruce,* 816a.

6. An even sharper critique of the song could be done while showing visuals or videos of Pol Pot and his ravaging of Cambodia or Hitler and his devastation of people in the Holocaust. I am indebted to Marie Gasau for this latter suggestion. I would not, however, use Sinatra in the same sequence.

7. Words by Bob Merrill and music by Jule Styne. Copyright 1963 and 1964.

8. Words by Stephen Sondheim and music by Leonard Bernstein. Copyright 1957.

9. Popular music is rich with possibilities for the basic structure of worship. This is also true of confession and forgiveness. In country music, for example, two of Kris Kristofferson's songs are very much on target. I think especially of "Why Me, Lord" and "Sunday Morning Coming Down."

10. This is Rollo May's formulation. See *Man's Search for Himself* (New York: Norton, 1953).

11. "One of Us," from the album *Relish*. Words and music by Eric Bazilian, ©1995. For a thematic guide to rock music, see Bob Machen, Peter Fornatale, and Bill Ayres, *The Rock Music Source Book* (Garden City, N.Y.: Anchor, 1980). For a more recent source of rock lyrics, see Scott Buchanan, ed., *Rock 'n Roll: The Famous Lyrics* (New York: HarperPerennial, 1994).

12. I am indebted to Marsha Morgan, professor of theater at Park College for this idea of a male and female voice, which she uses in liturgies to depict the voice of God.

13. From *Requiem*, music by Andrew Lloyd Webber, copyright 1995.

14. In developing alternative worship services see *Come Celebrate! A Guide for Planning Contemporary Worship*.

SELECT BIBLIOGRAPHY

Adams, Doug. *Congregational Dancing in Christian Worship.* San Francisco: The Sharing Company, 1971.

Adorno, Theodor W. *Introduction to the Sociology of Music,* translated by W. V. Blomster. New York: Seabury, 1976.

————. "On Popular Music." In *On Record: Rock, Pop and the Written Word,* edited by Simon Frith and Andrew Goodwin. New York: Pantheon, 1990.

————. "On the Fetish-Character in Music and the Regression of Listening." In *The Essential Frankfurt School Reader,* edited by Andrew Arato and Eike Gebhardt. New York: Continuum, 1982.

————. "Perennial Fashion—Jazz," in *Prizms,* translated by Samuel Weber and Shierry Weber. Cambridge, Mass.: MIT Press, 1981.

Anyanwu, Chukwulozie. "Sound As Ultimate Reality and Meaning: The Mode of Knowing Reality in African Thought," *Ultimate Reality and Meaning,* 10, no. 1 (March 1987).

Apple, Michael W., ed. *Cultural and Economic Reproduction in Education: Essays on Class, Ideology and the State.* London: Routledge and Kegan Paul, 1982.

Attali, Jacques. *Noise: The Political Economy of Music,* translated by Brian Massumi. Minneapolis: University of Minnesota Press, 1985.

Bakhtin, Mikhail. *Rabelais and His World.* Bloomington: Indiana University Press, 1984.

Bartlett, John. *Familiar Quotations.* Toronto: Little, Brown and Company, 1968. A poem by William Ernest Henley, *Echoes IV, In Memoriam R. T. Hamilton Bruce.*

Baudrillard, Jean. *Simulations.* Translated by Paul Foss, Paul Patton, and Philip Beitchman. New York: Semiotext(e), Inc., 1983.

Beniger, J. R. *The Control Revolution: Technological and Economic Origins of the Information Society.* Cambridge, Mass.: Harvard University Press, 1986.

Blacking, John. *Music, Culture, & Experience: Selected Papers of John Blacking.* Edited by Reginald Byron. Chicago: University of Chicago Press, 1995.

Bourdieu, Pierre. *Distinction: A Social Critique of the Judgement of Taste.* Translated by Richard Nice. Cambridge, Mass.: Harvard University Press, 1984.

Brook, James, and Iain A. Boal, eds. *Resisting the Virtual Life: The Culture and Politics of Information.* San Francisco: City Lights, 1995.

Bufwack, Mary A., and Robert K. Oermann. *Finding Her Voice: The Saga of Women in Country Music.* New York: Crown, 1993.

Bultman, Bethany. *Redneck Heaven: Protrait of a Vanishing Culture.* New York: Bantam, 1996.

Burnett, Ron. *Cultures of Vision: Images, Media and the Imaginary.* Bloomington: Indiana University Press, 1995.

Classen, Constance. *Worlds of Sense: Exploring the Senses in History and Across Cultures.* New York: Routledge, 1993.

Classen, Constance, David Howes, and Anthony Synnott. *Aroma: The Cultural History of Smell.* New York: Routledge, 1994.

Costa, Ruy O.,ed. *One Faith, Many Cultures: Inculturation, Indigenization, and Contextualization.* Maryknoll, N.Y.: Orbis, 1988.

Dawn, Marva J. *Reaching Out Without Dumbing Down: A Theology of Worship for the Turn-of-the-Century Culture.* Grand Rapids, Mich.: Eerdmans, 1995.

Debord, Guy. *The Society of the Spectacle.* Detroit: Black and Ted, 1976.

Deleuze, Gilles, and Felix Guattari. *A Thousand Plateaus: Capitalism and Schizophrenia.* Translated by Brian Massumi, 310–50. Minneapolis: University of Minnesota Press, 1987.

Dines, Gail, and Jean M. Humez, eds. *Gender, Race and Class in Media: A Text-Reader.* Thousand Oaks, Calif. : Sage Publications, 1995.

Durkheim, Emile. *The Division of Labor.* Translated by George Simpson. New York: The Free Press, 1964.

————. *The Elementary Forms of Religious Life.* Translated by Joseph Ward Swain. New York: Collier, 1961.

Eco, Umberto. "Towards a Semiotic Inquiry into the Television Message." In *Communication Studies: An Introductory Reader,* edited by John Corner and Jeremy Hawthorn. London: Edward Arnold, 1980.

Eisenstein, Elizabeth L. *The Printing Press As an Agent of Change.* Cambridge: Cambridge University Press, 1979.

Ewen, Stuart. *All Consuming Images: The Politics of Style in Contemporary Culture.* New York: Basic, 1988.

Fisk, John. *Reading the Popular.* London: Routledge, 1989.

————. *Understanding Popular Culture.* London: Routledge, 1989.

Fisk, John, and John Hartley. *Reading Television.* London: Methuen, 1978.

Fore, William F. *Mythmakers: Gospel, Culture and the Media.* New York: Friendship Press, 1990.

————. *Television and Religion: The Shaping of Faith, Values and Culture.* Minneapolis: Augsburg, 1987.

Foucault, Michel. *Power/Knowledge: Selected Interviews & Other Writings, 1972–1977.* Edited by Colin Gordon. New York: Pantheon, 1980.

Frith, Simon. *Music for Pleasure: Essays in the Sociology of Pop.* New York: Routledge, 1988.

Geertz, Clifford. *The Interpretation of Cultures.* New York: Basic, 1973.

Gitlin, Todd, ed. *Watching Television: A Pantheon Guide to Popular Culture.* New York: Pantheon, 1986.

Gittins, Anthony J. *Bread for the Journey: The Mission of Transformation and the Transformation of Mission.* Maryknoll, N.Y.: Orbis, 1993.

————. *Gifts and Strangers: Meeting the Challenge of Inculturation.* New York: Paulist, 1989.

Goethals, Gregory. *The Electronic Golden Calf: Images, Religion, and the Making of Meaning.* Cambridge, Mass.: Cowley Press, 1990.

Greenfield, Patricia Marks. *Mind and Media: The Effects of Television, Video Games, and Computers.* Cambridge, Mass.: Harvard University Press, 1984.

Grossberg, Lawrence. "Is Anybody Listening? Does Anybody Care?: On Talking About 'The State of Rock.' " In *Microphone Fiends: Youth Music and Youth Culture,* edited by Andrew Ross and Tricia Rose. New York: Routledge, 1994.

Guralnick, Peter. *Last Train to Memphis: The Rise of Elvis Presley.* New York: Little, Brown and Company, 1994.

————. *Sweet Soul Music: Rhythm and Blues and the Southern Dream of Freedom.* New York: Harper & Row, 1986.

Halberstam, David. *October 1964.* New York: Villard, 1994.

Hart, Mickey. *Drumming at the Edge of Magic.* San Francisco: Harper, 1990.

Hauerwas, Stanley. *The Peaceable Kingdom: A Primer in Christian Ethics.* Notre Dame: Notre Dame University Press, 1983.

Havel, Vaclav. *Living in Truth: Twenty-two Essays Published on the Occasion of the Award of the Erasmus Prize to Vaclav Havel.* Edited by Jan Vladislav. London: Faber & Faber, 1986.

Hebdige, Dick. *Subculture: The Meaning of Style.* New York: Routledge, 1979.

Hoge, Dean R., Benton Johnson, and Donald A. Luidens. *Vanishing Boundaries: The Religion of Mainline Protestant Baby Boomers.* Louisville: Westminster/John Knox, 1994.

Hoover, Stewart M. *Mass Media Religion: The Social Sources of the Electronic Church.* Beverly Hills, Calif.: Sage, 1988.

Innis, Harold. *The Bias of Communication.* Toronto: University of Toronto Press, 1964.

————. *Changing Concepts of Time.* Toronto: University of Toronto Press, 1952.

————. *Empire and Communication.* Oxford: Clarendon, 1950.

Jenks, Chris, ed. *Visual Culture.* London: Routledge, 1995.

Johns, Mark D. "The Rhetoric of Secondary Orality in Christian Homiletics: The Effects of the Electronic Media on Preaching." Master's thesis, University of Northern Iowa, December 1995.

Kellner, Douglas. *Television and the Crisis of Democracy.* Boulder, Col.: Westview, 1990.

Kelly, Linda. *Deadheads: Stories from Fellow Artists, Friends, and Followers of the Grateful Dead.* New York: Carol Publishing Co., A Citadel Press Book, 1995.

Kress, Gunther, and Theo van Leeuwen, *Reading Images: The Grammar of Visual Design.* London: Routledge, 1996.

Lenski, Gerhard E. *Power and Privilege: A Theory of Stratification.* New York: McGraw-Hill, 1966.

Leppert, Richard, and Susan McClary, eds. *Music and Society.* Cambridge: Cambridge University Press, 1987.

Levine, Lawrence W. *Highbrow/Lowbrow: The Emergence of Cultural Hierarchy in America.* Cambridge, Mass.: Harvard University Press, 1988.

Limburg, Val E. *Electronic Media Ethics.* Boston: Focal Press, 1994.

Lippman, Edward. *A History of Western Musical Aesthetics.* Lincoln: University of Nebraska Press, 1992.

Lipsitz, George. *Class and Culture in Cold War America.* South Hadley, Mass.: Bergin & Garvey, 1982.

————. *Time Passages: Collective Memory and American Popular Culture.* Minneapolis: University of Minnesota Press, 1990.

Lyotard, Jean-Francois. *Driftworks.* New York: Semiotext(e), 1984.

————. *Discours, Figure.* Paris: Klincksieck, 1971.

McClary, Susan. *Feminine Endings: Music, Gender, and Sexuality.* Minneapolis: University of Minnesota Press, 1991.

McClary, Susan, and Richard Leppert, eds. *Music and Society: The Politics of Composition, Performance and Reception.* Cambridge: Cambridge University Press, 1989.

McGrath, Tom. *MTV: The Making of a Revolution.* Philadelphia: Running Press, 1996.

MacIntyre, Alasdair. *After Virtue: A Study in Moral Theory.* 2nd ed. Notre Dame, Ind.: Notre Dame University Press, 1984.

————. *Whose Justice—Whose Rationality.* Notre Dame, Ind.: Notre Dame University Press, 1988.

McLuhan, Marshal. *Understanding Media.* New York: The New American Library, 1964.

Malone, Bill C. *Country Music USA: A Fifty Year History.* Austin: The University of Texas Press, 1968.

Messaris, Paul. *Visual Literacy: Image, Mind, and Reality.* Boulder, Col.: Westview, 1994.

Meyrowitz, Joshua. *No Sense of Place: The Impact of Electronic Media on Social Behavior.* London: Oxford University Press, 1985.

Middleton, Richard. *Studying Popular Music.* Philadelphia: Open University Press, 1990.

Myers, Helen, ed. *Ethnomusicology: An Introduction.* New York: W. W. Norton, 1992.

Ong, Walter. *Orality and Literacy.* London: Routledge, 1982.

————. *The Presence of the Word.* Minneapolis: University of Minnesota, 1967.

————. *Rhetoric, Romance, and Technology: Studies in the Interaction of Expression and Culture.* Ithaca, N.Y.: Cornell University Press, 1971.

Postman, Neil. *Amusing Ourselves to Death.* New York: Penguin, 1985.

————. *Technopoly: The Surrender of Culture to Technology.* New York: Vintage, 1992.

Penny, Simon, ed. *Critical Issues in Electronic Media.* Albany: State University of New York Press, 1995.

Real, Michael R. *Mass-Mediated Culture.* Englewood Cliffs, N.J.: Prentice-Hall, 1977.

Roof, Wade Clark. *A Generation of Seekers: The Spiritual Journeys of the Baby Boom Generation.* San Francisco: HarperSanFrancisco, 1993.

Rorty, Richard. *Philosophy and the Mirror of Nature.* Princeton: Princeton University Press, 1979.

Rose, Tricia. *Black Noise: Rap Music and Black Culture in Contemporary America.* Hanover, N.H.: Wesleyan University Press, 1994.

Ross, Andrew, and Tricia Rose, eds. *Microphone Fiends: Youth Music and Youth Culture.* New York: Routledge, 1994.

Said, Edward W. *Orientalism.* Harmondsworth: Penguin, 1985.

————. *The World, the Text, and the Critic.* Cambridge, Mass.: Harvard University Press, 1983.

Sample, Tex. *White Soul: Country Music, the Church, and Working People.* Nashville: Abingdon, 1996.

Schiller, Herbert. *Information and the Crisis Economy.* Norwood, N.J.: Ablex, 1984.

Schultze, Quinton J., Roy M. Anker, James D. Bratt, William D. Romanski, John W. Worst, and Lambert Zuidervaart. *Dancing in the Dark: Youth, Popular Culture, and the Electronic Media.* Grand Rapids, Mich.: Eerdmans, 1991.

Smith, Anthony. *The Geopolitics of Information: How Western Culture Dominates the World.* London: Oxford University Press, 1980.

Smith, J. Walker, and Ann Clurman. *Rocking the Ages: The Yankelovich Report on Generational Marketing.* New York: HarperBusiness, 1997.

Snyder, Howard A. *EarthCurrents: The Struggle for the World's Soul.* Nashville: Abingdon, 1995.

Sorlin, Pierre. *Mass Media.* London: Routledge, 1994.

Taylor, Mark C., and Esa Saarinen. *Imagologies: Media Philosophy.* London: Routledge, 1994.

Tester, Keith. *Media, Culture and Morality.* London: Routledge, 1994.

Tirro, Frank. *Jazz: A History.* New York: Norton, 1977.

Walser, Robert. *Running with the Devil: Power, Gender, and Madness in Heavy Metal Music*. Hanover, N.H.: Wesleyan University Press, 1993.

Ward, Ed, Geoffrey Stokes, and Ken Tucker. *Rock of Ages: The Rolling Stone History of Rock and Roll*. New York: Rolling Stone Press, 1986.

Weiss, Piero, and Richard Taruskin, eds. *Music in the Western World: A History in Documents*. New York: Schirmer, 1984.

Wexler, Jerry, and David Ritz, *Rhythm and the Blues: A Life in American Music*. New York: St. Martin's, 1993.

White, Susan J. *Christian Worship and Technological Change*. Nashville: Abingdon, 1994.

Williams, Raymond. *The Sociology of Culture*. New York: Schocken, 1981.

————. *Television: Technology and Cultural Form*. New York: Schocken, 1975.

————. *Writing in Society*. London: Verso, 1983.

Williams, Roger M. *Sing a Sad Song: The Life of Hank Williams*. 2nd ed. Chicago: University of Illinois Press, 1981.

Wray, Matt, and Annalee Newitz, eds. *White Trash: Race and Class in America*. New York: Routledge, 1997.

Zill, Nicolas, and John Robinson. "The Generation X Difference." *American Demographics* (April 1995), 24–29, 32–33.

INDEX

LINCOLN CHRISTIAN COLLEGE AND SEMINARY 95296

261.52
SA192
c. 1

3 4711 00165 8840